National Council for the Social Studies

# TEACHING

## THE COLLEGE, CAREER, AND CIVIC LIFE (C3) FRAMEWORK:
### EXPLORING INQUIRY-BASED INSTRUCTION IN SOCIAL STUDIES

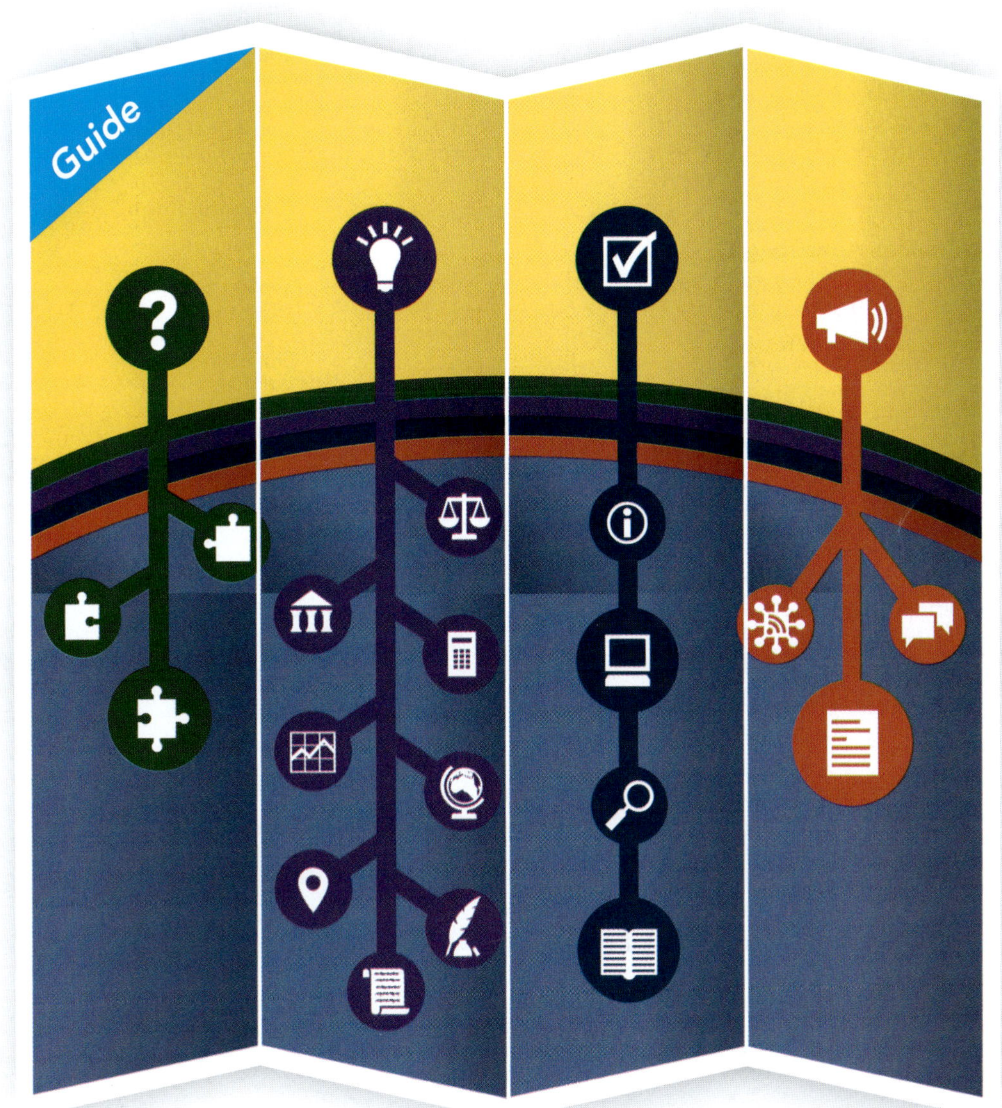

Edited by

## KATHY SWAN & JOHN LEE
with Rebecca Mueller & Stephen Day

**NCSS**
**Bulletin 114**

# National Council for the Social Studies

8555 Sixteenth Street • Suite 500 • Silver Spring, Maryland 20910

## NCSS BOARD OF DIRECTORS, 2014-2015




NCSS EXECUTIVE DIRECTOR — **Susan Griffin**

NCSS DIRECTOR OF PUBLICATIONS — **Michael Simpson**

DESIGN — **Inquiring Minds** Monica Snellings and DK Holland

PRODUCTION — **Cowan Creative** Gene Cowan

NCSS EDITORIAL STAFF ON THIS PUBLICATION — **Michael Simpson, Jennifer Bauduy, Steven Lapham**

NCSS is grateful to the fifteen institutions contributing to this book for permission to reproduce their logos on the back cover of this publication.

ISBN: 978-0-87986-108-7

# Table of CONTENTS

# PREFACE



Inquiry, as an approach to teaching and learning social studies, is not new. Inquiry was on the minds of the educators who created social studies as a school subject over 100 years ago and has in many ways been a part of social studies every since. Building from Dewey's notion that people develop thinking skills by wrestling with the "conditions of a problem," to Jerome Bruner's focus on discovery learning (Bruner, 1960) and through to the C3 Framework,* inquiry has been a consistent ambition of social studies.

The C3 Framework approaches inquiry from the unique perspective of standards. While the C3 Framework includes a set of indicators setting forth what students should learn at the end of four grade bands, the real innovation is represented in the design of the Inquiry Arc. It is through the Inquiry Arc and the related four dimensions of the Framework that inquiry takes shape.

The C3 Framework calls for students to demonstrate competency within a disciplined inquiry. This process, more recursive than prescriptive, suggests that students move along four important steps or dimensions:

1. Developing questions and planning inquiries;
2. Applying disciplinary concepts and tools;
3. Evaluating sources and using evidence; and
4. Communicating conclusions and taking informed action.

This Inquiry Arc creates a parallel set of expectations for teachers in what Grant (2013) calls an Instructional Arc, which takes its cues from the C3 Framework. Grant sees this *Instructional Arc* as "a lesson and unit planning approach that foregrounds the use of teacher- and student-developed questions" (p. 325). Teachers will need to be intentional about making space in the curriculum, selecting sources, building in scaffolding, and incorporating related assessments in order to support students in this process. Following this Instructional Arc, if students are to marshal evidence when making an argument, teachers will need to provide experiences that allow students to practice gathering information from sources and making claims supported with evidence.

Teaching within this inquiry model is ambitious and gratifying, but at the same time, presents some daunting challenges. Teachers often struggle to find the time for inquiry, given the required scope and sequence of many social studies courses. The incredible breadth of content that social studies teachers have to deal with can sometimes eclipse the best of pedagogical intentions. And if teachers conquer that challenge, there is always

---

* See National Council for the Social Studies (NCSS), *The College, Career, and Civic Life (C3) Framework for Social Studies State Standards: Guidance for Enhancing the Rigor of K-12 Civics, Economics, Geography, and History* (Silver Spring, MD: NCSS, 2013). The C3 Framework is available online at www.socialstudies.org/C3. A hard copy, along with introductory explanatory chapters, is included in the NCSS Bulletin, *Social Studies for the Next Generation: Purposes, Practices, and Implications of the College, Career, and Civic Life (C3) Framework for Social Studies State Standards* (Silver Spring, MD: NCSS, 2013). The pagination of the C3 Framework is identical in both the online and the hard copies.

the complexity of the inquiry itself. How do we work with students to craft questions that can spark and sustain an inquiry? What, if any, amount of background knowledge is needed before initiating an inquiry? How can a teacher strike the right equilibrium between students practicing disciplinary literacy skills and having a meaningful content experience? And, in what ways can students bridge these academic inquiries into civic action? At the end of the day, inquiry is worth the effort but can be challenging for even the most seasoned and talented of teachers!

To begin chipping away at these challenges, we engaged fifteen of the best social studies curricular organizations in taking the "C3 Instructional Arc Challenge." The partners were asked to create lessons that would encompass the whole of the C3 Inquiry Arc, from questioning to action, and we asked that each lesson would take between 2-5 days of instruction. The authors were charged with finding ways to have students collaborate, to practice disciplinary literacy skills, to creatively present their findings, and to do so within a meaningful content experience at all grade bands from K-2 to 9-12. We see these chapters/lessons as a guide for teachers to implement and replicate the C3 Instructional Arc within their own classroom. The book focuses on topics that are central to social studies taught in schools across the country, providing teachers with insight into how the arc can be realistically integrated into existing curricula.

We would like to extend our sincere appreciation for the dedication and commitment each of our partners has shown in bringing this Bulletin to life. We recognize that we were sticklers in many ways, and thus appreciate the persistence and willingness each of the organizations showed in getting these chapters right. We are humbled to work with such an impressive array of organizations and colleagues and to follow in the collaborative spirit of the C3 Framework:

- Bill of Rights Institute
- The Colonial Williamsburg Foundation
- Facing History and Ourselves
- Federal Reserve Bank of St. Louis
- Gilder Lehrman Institute of American History
- Library of Congress
- Mikva Challenge
- National Archives
- National Constitution Center
- National Geographic Society
- National History Day
- National Museum of American History
- National Museum of the American Indian
- Newseum
- University of Delaware Center for Economic Education

We are grateful to the C3 Teachers group (http://C3teachers.org) for working through the instructional design ideas presented in this Bulletin.

We would also like to thank Monica Snellings and DK Holland of Inquiring Minds for once again breathing creative life into the pages of a book on the C3 Framework and demonstrating, once more, that form is often as important as function. We are also grateful to Gene Cowan, of Cowan Creative, for directing the production of this book.

Together with these partners, we hope that we have created a resource that will help teachers hone their inquiry practices in teaching students to wrestle with ideas, events, and issues that are so central to a robust social studies education.

**Kathy Swan, John Lee, Rebecca Mueller and Stephen Day**

# ABOUT THE EDITORS

**Kathy Swan** is an associate professor of social studies education at the University of Kentucky. She was the Lead Writer and Project Director of the College, Career, and Civic Life ("C3") Framework for Social Studies State Standards, and is co-director of C3teachers.org.

**John Lee** is an associate professor of social studies education at North Carolina State University. He was a Contributing Writer and Senior Consultant of the College, Career, and Civic Life (C3) Framework for Social Studies State Standards, and is co-director of C3teachers.org.

**Rebecca Mueller** is a National Board Certified Teacher who is currently pursuing her doctoral degree at the University of Kentucky with a focus on student questioning.

**Stephen Day** is the director of the Center for Economic Education at Virginia Commonwealth University.


**REFERENCES**

Bruner, J. (1960). *The Process of Education* (p. 33). Cambridge: Harvard University Press.

Dewey, J. (1916). *Democracy and Education: An Introduction to the Philosophy of Education* (p. 188). New York: The Macmillan Company.

Grant, S. G. (2013). "From Inquiry Arc to Instructional Practice: The Potential of the C3 Framework." *Social Education* 77 (6), pp. 322–326, 351.


The URLs for resources on the websites that are cited in this book by authors from the contributing institutions were accessed in September and October 2014. Readers can usually also locate the resources by entering identifying information into the search engines on the websites of these institutions.

# CHAPTER 1

# Should Citizenship Be **Revolutionary?**

**The Colonial Williamsburg Foundation**

The newly adopted Declaration of Independence was read aloud in Williamsburg, Virginia on July 25, 1776.

**The Colonial Williamsburg Foundation, Department of Education Outreach**

| **C3 Disciplinary Focus** | **C3 Inquiry Focus** | **Content Topic** |
|---|---|---|
| U.S. History, Civics | Gathering information from sources, using evidence, and taking informed action | Interpreting the nation's founding principles, enshrined in the Declaration of Independence |

**C3 Focus Indicators**

**D1:** Explain how a question represents key ideas in the field. (D1.1.6-8)

**D2:** Analyze ideas and principles contained in the founding documents of the United States, and explain how they influence the social and political system. (D2.Civ.8.6-8)

**D3:** Identify evidence that draws information from multiple sources to support claims, noting evidentiary limitations. (D3.3.6-8)

**D4:** Apply a range of deliberative and democratic procedures to make decisions and take actions in their classrooms and schools, and in out-of-school civic contexts. (D4.8.6-8)

*This lesson can also be adapted for use in grades 9–12 to achieve the comparable C3 objectives for those grade levels.*

| **Grade Level** | **Resources** | **Time Required** |
|---|---|---|
| 6–8 and higher | Resources cited in this chapter; the Colonial Williamsburg Teacher Community website* | 3 to 5 class periods |

* A more detailed lesson plan and resources relating to this chapter will be posted on Colonial Williamsburg's Teacher Community, http://teachers.history.org.

# Introduction and Connections to the C3 Framework

Active citizenship requires more than a few rote displays of patriotism: casting a vote on Election Day, flying the flag, or standing for the national anthem at a ballgame. It must be about training our young people to actively contribute to their communities. The history classroom has a central role to play. Our shared past is not a static collection of facts to be memorized, much less bronzed heroes to worship. It lives, and we must help students discover how the national experience connects with their lives and their futures.

The American Revolution is the defining event in American history, the crucible in which all our struggles for freedom and equality have been formed. Its significance extends beyond the successful war for independence waged by the American colonies against Great Britain. It was radical because Americans rejected their role as subjects and, with it, notions of inherited wealth and station. The Declaration of Independence set in motion an enduring debate that continues today about what our core democratic principles are and how they should be realized.

Students should have the opportunity to be active participants in this debate, because it goes to the very heart of what it means to "do" history and, moreover, what it means to be an American. What essential values do we cherish? What is their relationship to the founding of our nation? How have the concrete meanings we attach to our founding principles changed over time? By analyzing the Declaration of Independence as a primary source, then comparing it to other documents that echo its key tenets, students can gain an effective understanding of how citizens have employed the core principles of our founding documents to drive historical change.

The classroom strategies proposed below aim to build historical content knowledge while honing "the critical thinking, problem solving, and collaborative skills needed for the workplace." (C3 Framework, p. 6) The heart of historical inquiry is the careful analysis of primary sources. Students will learn to think like historians by interrogating texts to construct meaning. But there is another step that is crucial: students must learn to find themselves in the nation's stories. They must learn that the care of the republic is entrusted to all citizens, not a select group of leaders.

Supporters of this idea "are bound by a common belief that our democratic republic will not sustain unless students are aware of their changing cultural and physical environments; know the past; read, write, and think deeply; and act in ways that promote the common good" (C3 Framework, p. 5). So as a culminating activity, we ask students to apply the principles and lessons of the Declaration of Independence in their own communities.

# Inquiry Arc

The Colonial Williamsburg Foundation's mission is "that the future may learn from the past," but what does that mean in practical terms? Our nation's history is not a straight line of greater progress and freedom. It has been an arduous journey, on a path illuminated by high principles we have often failed to realize. In order to continue to create "a more perfect union," we need to accurately understand where we have been.

It begins with the American Revolution, which was much more than a military conflict. The Revolution is central to our identity as Americans not just because it marks our founding. It also represents the toppling of a world predicated on inherited privilege in favor of one based on individual rights under a constitution—in the words of President Lincoln—"of the people, by the people, and for the people."

This lesson explores how Americans honor our revolutionary legacy. Do the principles enshrined in the Declaration of Independence have fixed meanings, or do they shift over time? Does being a good citizen mean protecting the integrity of our founding documents, or challenging them for any perceived shortcomings? Ultimately, students must weigh in with their own answers to the question: Should citizenship be revolutionary?

In Dimension 1, students begin by parsing the compelling question and examining the terms "revolutionary" and "citizenship," in order to generate a series of supporting questions to support the larger inquiry. In Dimension 2, students engage in a close reading of one of our "revolutionary" documents, the Declaration of Independence, to analyze its many facets and gain a deeper understanding of our founding principles. Dimension 3 asks students to look at a variety of documents throughout our history that echo the Declaration to examine how the definition of "citizenship" has been reinterpreted over time. Students will use these experiences as building blocks so that during Dimension 4, students can answer "Should Citizenship Be Revolutionary?" and apply it to the real world.


## Dimension 1: Developing Questions and Planning Inquiries

Americans have a complex relationship with the Declaration of Independence. Frequently we treat it as a pillar of undisputed wisdom, passed down from a uniquely enlightened founding generation. At the same time, we are mindful that eighteenth-century notions of freedom and equality, for example, were very different from our own. We can inject new life into the Declaration of Independence by embracing this paradox.

Students in the social studies classroom are being introduced to a litany of dates, events and heroes associated with the republic's founding. But we can breathe new life into the story by helping students to understand that our Revolutionary principles live on today. But how, exactly?

We begin with an ongoing historical debate that lies at the heart of our identity as Americans. It is a debate that any educated citizen should feel empowered to participate in—namely, *just how revolutionary was the American Revolution?* Historians examine endless pieces of evidence in search of the answer.

They generally agree on a few key facts. The Declaration of Independence was a major milestone in the advance of self-government as a potential reality. The destruction of hierarchy represented a dramatic departure from typical 18th-century government. But placing power in the hands of the people was regarded with great suspicion, even by many who strongly supported the American rebellion against Britain, and real social change was slow in coming.

If we accept the premise that the Declaration of Independence was both a revolutionary document and the source of our citizenship, did citizenship continue to be related to revolutionary change? Students will analyze the Declaration of Independence and related texts in search of the answer. They will be equipped to "explain how a question represents key ideas in the field." (D1.1.6-8)

The next step is to define our terms. Use a class discussion to ask: What does "citizenship" mean? What do we mean by "revolutionary"? Create a word cloud for each on the board or on a worksheet and discuss the variety of interpretations students have for each word.

Consult dictionary definitions for each term and see how they compare. For example:

**CITIZENSHIP** (n.) the state of being vested with the rights, privileges, and duties of a citizen.

**REVOLUTIONARY** (adj.) of, pertaining to, characterized by, or of the nature of a revolution, or a sudden, complete, or marked change.

Once students have a clear grasp of the words, ask students what information they will need as evidence. What clues would they look for in a text? How will the dictionary definitions guide their inquiry? Generate a short list of supporting questions that will help guide the class as it moves through each of the dimensions.

Beginning to understand the constellation of meanings attached to these terms is a necessary first step in preparing to answer the compelling question, "Should Citizenship Be Revolutionary?" They will be able to begin assessing historical evidence against the rhetoric of the Declaration of Independence.

## Dimension 2: Connections to Disciplinary Tools and Concepts

### "We have it in our power to begin the world over again."

Thomas Paine's words were prophetic, coming early in 1776, mere months before the American colonies declared their independence from Britain. The Declaration abruptly tossed aside centuries of hierarchical rule in favor of an experiment in self-government. Citizens took the place of monarchs and hereditary privilege. The Declaration was revolutionary precisely because it did represent starting over.

Americans rightly revere the founding generation for what it set in motion. But the question for citizens today is how to be good caretakers of our revolutionary inheritance. Does it mean preserving what was won and protecting against changes that might seem radical? Or does the nature of our founding obligate each generation "to begin the world over again"? How can we adjust to modern realities while maintaining our most cherished principles?

Time and again, as a people we return to the Declaration of Independence for answers. We want to know that the nation is headed in the right direction. How well are we achieving the promise of "life, liberty and the pursuit of happiness"? Do we find "absolute tyranny" in our government? What does "all men are created equal" mean in practice?

To find the answers we seek, we need to interpret the Declaration through the essential and supporting questions developed in Dimension 1. We begin by breaking the document down into its key components. This analysis of ideas and principles trains students to employ the text evidence that is essential when comparing the Declaration to other documents. The process might look something like this:

**READ** the Declaration of Independence in full. Ask students to underline or list key words and phrases that relate to important principles.

**DISCUSS** what the Declaration of Independence means. For example:
- What is its structure? (Could you make an outline?)
- Who were the authors? What was their point of view?
- What fundamental principles does it advance?
- How was citizenship revolutionary in 1776?
- Whose points of view are left out or minimized?

**HYPOTHESIZE** whether the Declaration has a static or changing meaning.
- What made the document revolutionary?
- Does it still have meaning today?
- What evidence (within the text or requiring additional research) would help to confirm your hypotheses?

After reading and discussing the Declaration of Independence as a class, students should understand that the Declaration was revolutionary not only because it was connected to a war for independence but also because it was the basis for toppling centuries-old notions of hierarchy. Students should also understand that this is what transformed the colonists from British subjects into American citizens.

An awareness that citizenship entails both rights and responsibilities will help students take the next step by analyzing other events in American history that help to answer the question "Should citizenship be revolutionary?" In this way, they will be prepared to "analyze ideas and principles contained in the founding documents of the United States, and explain how they influence the social and political system." (D2.Civ.8.6-8)

## Dimension 3: Evaluating Sources and Using Evidence

The Declaration of Independence was a document of its time but applies to many different circumstances. Its 1776 audience interpreted it within the context of the Revolutionary War. Later generations have seized on particular elements in order to argue for new ways to understand and apply its principles. But it has never spoken for itself; its meaning is contingent and contested.

Citizens have used the Declaration to advance their own perspectives. They have capitalized on its authority as a founding document to voice grievances in their own times, on issues ranging from slavery to women's rights to Native American sovereignty. In all cases the question comes down to: How do we achieve its promise? And in so doing, are we accomplishing a revolutionary act?

By comparing the Declaration of Independence with later documents that invoked the language of the Declaration for new purposes, we can come to terms with how its meaning has evolved and been appropriated by different groups of citizens, for different purposes. For example, Elizabeth Cady Stanton extended its affirmation of equality to women at the Seneca Falls Convention in 1848:

| Declaration of Independence | Elizabeth Cady Stanton, Seneca Falls Convention |
| --- | --- |
| all men are created equal | all men **and women** are created equal |

Ask students to answer the following questions:

- What points of view are represented? How are they different?
  *The Declaration specifies equality for "all men." Stanton has added women. One question is why there was no mention of women in the first place. Was it because they were not included or because the phrasing was meant to mean "mankind"? In either case Stanton is making a claim for the inclusion of women.*

- What values are highlighted?
  *Stanton wants **equality** extended to women. She also wants more **unity**, which can be achieved by treating men and women as equal citizens.*

- What additional information do we need to understand the history behind the quotation?
  *We need to understand what rights of citizenship and political participation men and women had in 1776 as well as at the time of the Seneca Falls Convention, and what additional rights women sought to gain more equality. We might also look at who else lacked political rights. African Americans, for example, also lacked the full rights of citizenship, which meant that African American women faced additional challenges.*

- Are Elizabeth Cady Stanton's actions an example of revolutionary citizenship? Why or why not?
  *Yes: Elizabeth Cady Stanton was revolutionary because the idea of political rights for women was a radical departure from the reality of the time and the intent of the founders. Such a change threatened major social upheaval.*
  *No: Elizabeth Cady Stanton worked within the political system by accepted means, such as political organization and petitioning. She sought to gain rights peacefully.*

Discuss findings with the whole class. You might decide to post the quotations, gradually building a timeline that would illustrate what issues were being highlighted at different times in our history. This could extend right into the present as the lesson develops.

Many other primary source documents make rights claims by echoing or invoking the Declaration. They include:

- William Lloyd Garrison on slavery, 1831
- Frederick Douglass, What to the slave is the 4th of July?, 1854
- Jacob Riis on poverty, 1902
- Eugene Debs on labor, 1916
- Emma Goldman on the military draft, 1917
- Dr. Martin Luther King, Jr.'s "I Have a Dream" speech, 1963
- Native American "Declaration of Continuing Independence," 1974
- Fredric Schroeder on the rights of blind Americans, 2007

These documents are accessible on Colonial Williamsburg's Teacher Community website at http://teachers.history.org. Having laid the groundwork of the lesson in the text of the Declaration, help students interrogate these other primary source documents in light of founding principles. For example, how have Americans defined "life, liberty and the pursuit of happiness"? "Created equal"? How have citizens tried to alter or amend our understanding of those values? Guide students to understand evolving interpretations are part of an enduring debate about democratic principles.

Guide students back to the essential question, "Should citizenship be revolutionary?" Encourage them to form explanations of how different generations of Americans devised new interpretations of founding principles that reflected changes in society since 1776. This requires students to combine their familiarity with the texts and historical context (typically provided by classroom lecture or secondary sources). Students formulate a thesis and support it with relevant evidence. If evidence is missing, they should note that as well. In this way, students will practice C3 Inquiry skills as they "identify evidence that draws information from multiple sources to support claims, noting evidentiary limitations." (D3.3.6-8)

## Dimension 4: Communicating Conclusions and Taking Informed Action

Every generation of citizens must decide for itself how our founding documents should be applied. Americans are not born with this knowledge; it must be learned. Having done the work of analyzing the Declaration through history, students become scholars of the Declaration of Independence, and in turn, scholars of American history. We should acknowledge the significance of that work. Instill the idea that by working through this series of historical questions, students are the worthy inheritors of our experiment in self-government.

Scholars—engaged participants in historical inquiry—are prepared to "apply a range of deliberative and democratic procedures to make decisions and take actions in their classrooms and schools, and in out-of-school civic contexts." (D4.8.6-8) Depending on available class time, there are several ways to work toward this goal.

Begin by looking at the word clouds that were created in Dimension 1. Ask students to answer the question, "Should Citizenship Be Revolutionary?" Ask students to share their thoughts in a class discussion. Based on the answers that are generated, any of the following activities might be used as assessments, but together they function as practical training for becoming engaged citizens.

**MY DECLARATION:** What would the Declaration of Independence look like if it were being written today? What should it look like? Students can work independently or in small groups to compose a modern declaration that reflects their own understanding of the nation's core principles. Students can adopt any of the different styles from the documents they have analyzed, or they can find their own voice. What is most important is for students to think about their rights and responsibilities in the community. Their "declaration" should be an expression of citizenship in a community. It doesn't have to be the nation. It might be their school, town, city, neighborhood, or church group, for example. Discuss whether their vision represents "revolutionary" citizenship. Why or why not?

**CLASS DECLARATIONS:** How do students learn to work together to build a consensus? Can we train them to work collaboratively on a scholarly enterprise with practical application? Bring students together in two miniature congresses to draft a modern declaration as described above. One group is composed of students who believe citizenship should be revolutionary; the other is made up of those students who believe we should be focused on preserving what we have already. Have each group compose their new declaration; then bring the class together to discuss their differences. The important thing is to create an environment in which the free and open exchange of ideas is possible, and disagreements are dealt with respectfully.

**CIVIC ACTION:** Can students effect real change in their communities today? Building on the class's declarations, find a real problem to tackle. What steps will help to achieve the principles set out in the declarations? What barriers stand in the way? This is not about the achievement of major change so much as it is training students in the tools of democracy. Write a letter to the editor. Circulate a petition. Lobby elected leaders. Volunteer for service in the community. Attend a meeting or hearing. Offer comments on local government initiatives.

Schools have no greater function than to educate citizens. If we educate our young people only to become good workers, there is no guarantee they will become good citizens. But if we educate them to be good citizens, they will become good workers—or good scientists, engineers, or teachers. We will have an effective workforce, because we will have good citizens. We will have strong communities, because we will have good citizens. And ultimately, it is engaged—and courageous—citizens who determine whether change should be revolutionary or not.

# About The Colonial Williamsburg Foundation

The Colonial Williamsburg Foundation operates the world's largest living history museum and is located in Williamsburg, Virginia—the restored 18th-century capital of Britain's largest, wealthiest, and most populous outpost of empire in the Americas. Our mission, first iterated by John D. Rockefeller, is "That the future may learn from the past." One of the ways we pursue that goal is by interpreting the American Revolution, and we believe the founding era should continue to inform our understanding and interpretation of subsequent events.

Our educational initiatives are built on the premise that there is an important connection between American history and our role as citizens: good history triggers engagement and commitment to citizenship.

Visit http://history.org/teach for more information on:
- The Virtual Republic
- *The Idea of America*™
- Quill Close Reading Series: Declaring Independence

*This chapter was prepared by the Colonial Williamsburg Department of Education Outreach. Its authors are: Bill Sullivan, History and Citizenship Editor; Gina DeAngelis, Senior Editor-Writer; Kelly Govain, Senior Coordinator of Teacher Development; William (Bill) Fetsko, Curriculum Consultant; and David Arehart, Production Associate. The copyright of this chapter is owned by The Colonial Williamsburg Foundation.*
*© The Colonial Williamsburg Foundation, 2014.*

# CHAPTER 2

# What Does **Liberty** Look Like?

**The Gilder Lehrman Institute of American History**

**The Gilder Lehrman Institute of American History**

| **C3 Disciplinary Focus** U.S. History, Civics | **C3 Inquiry Focus** Evaluating sources and using evidence | **Content Topic** American symbols of liberty |
| --- | --- | --- |

**C3 Focus Indicators**

**D1:** Make connections between supporting questions and compelling questions. (D1.4.K–2)

**D1:** Identify disciplinary ideas associated with a compelling question. (D1.2.K-2)

**D2:** Describe democratic principles such as equality, fairness, and respect for legitimate authority and rules. (D2.Civ.8.K–2)

**D3:** Gather relevant information from one or two sources while using the origin and structure to guide the selection. (D3.1.K–2)

**D4:** Present a summary of an argument using print, oral, and digital technologies. (D4.3.K–2)

| **Grade Level** K-2 | **Resources** Resources cited in the chapter; Gilder Lehrman website | **Time Required** 3 class periods |
| --- | --- | --- |

# Introduction and Connections to the C3 Framework

*What does liberty look like?* Every day, Americans encounter images and symbols that shape their individual and communal identities and contribute to their contextual understanding of everything from the products they buy to the foundational philosophies, ideas, and themes that lie at the heart of American life. Through iconic symbols, Americans develop understanding of the language and activity of democracy, as well as the experiences that build context for everyday life and strong, active, and effective participation in American society.

When teachers of social studies look to utilize primary sources in the classroom, many turn to great documents from American history as a way of introducing their students to the language, tenor, and dialogue that compose the intricacies of our nation's heritage and history. The craft of the historian requires a deep contemplation of the past as well as the development and use of sound evidence—in the form of firsthand accounts, primary documents, and secondary sources—to determine what happened in an event, how it happened, and what its immediate and historic circumstances and results were socially, politically, and economically.

When working with lower elementary-grade social studies classrooms, unique challenges arise. Because young learners do not yet possess fully formed language fluency and may not understand the complex vocabulary of primary historic texts, the teachers of the youngest learners face great barriers in using the traditional tools of the historian. Using the resources of the Gilder Lehrman Institute for American History's Collection, this chapter takes a document-based approach to teaching inquiry-based lessons by engaging students with the fundamental documents of American history while enhancing discipline-specific literacy skills. The lessons in this chapter allow early elementary students to dig into the fundamental aspects and vocabulary of symbolism and prompt them to engage in a critical discussion of "American Symbols." These lessons teach K-2 students about significant artifacts of American heritage and help students take deep dives into what could be their first exposure to a learning process embedded in historical inquiry as outlined in the C3 Framework.

# Inquiry Arc

This chapter explores how teachers of lower elementary grades can use a document-based approach to instruction, integrating primary sources and the dimensions of the C3 Framework to bring social studies to life for young learners. In Dimension 1, students will begin examining a supporting question for the larger inquiry into the nature and purpose of symbols and the notion of liberty. In Dimensions 2 and 3, students expand their historical understanding of the United States of America and American symbols by learning to "read" several symbols, including the Flag of the United States of America, and the Statue of Liberty. A subsequent related activity could focus on the Great Seal of the United States. In Dimension 4, students communicate their understanding of the compelling question "What does liberty look like?" by constructing a classroom symbol of liberty and sharing it with others.

### Dimension 1: Developing Questions and Planning Inquiries

What is a symbol? This seemingly simple question will frame students' understanding as they begin the journey of investigating some of America's most recognizable icons, the American Flag, the Statue of Liberty, and the Great Seal of the United States of America. This initial step in the C3 Inquiry Arc will allow students to participate in an inquiry into symbols that are central to American life, culture, and heritage and work their way towards the anchor question: What does liberty look like? With this significant question in mind, the starting point of the Inquiry Arc will push students to consider that even America's most visible symbols are those that require interpretation and discussion.

Symbols are important in your young students' lives; they just may not recognize the fact until you make it explicit for them. The question of "What is a symbol?" will become a supporting question for the students as they begin to see how often they use symbols in their everyday lives. For example, show the students a picture of a stoplight and ask them what the red, green, and yellow lights mean. Those colors are symbols for stop, go, and caution. These symbols keep them safe. Another example would be a + or = symbol in a math problem. Have the students draw all of the symbols that they can think of that they use in their lives: a happy face, ☺, a walk/don't walk on the street corner, even the drawing of a boy or girl on the restroom door!

These foundational discussions will lead to an understanding not only of the role of symbols but of the importance in the symbolism of the American Flag, the Statue of Liberty, and the Great Seal of the United States. By spending time with the supporting questions for "What is a Symbol?" at the beginning of the inquiry, students will begin to "make connections between supporting questions and compelling questions." (D1.4.K–2)

Before engaging in the inquiry, students will also need time to consider the supporting question, "What is liberty?" Start with a discussion of "What is liberty?" Is it the idea that we can do whatever we want when we want? What if what we want to do hurts others? What if what we want interferes with what someone else wants? Liberty is the power to choose, think, and act for oneself. That includes making choices that do what is best not only for oneself but for others as well. You might also have students consider "liberty" through other senses. For example, students can contemplate the sounds of liberty by listening to songs that include "liberty" in the lyrics (e.g., "The Liberty Song," "My Country, 'Tis of Thee") or listening to famous quotes that address liberty (e.g., "We hold these truths to be self-evident: that all men are created equal; that they are endowed by their Creator with certain unalienable rights; that among these are life, liberty, and the pursuit of happiness," from the Declaration of Independence).

As students begin working with the terms and ideas within the inquiry question, they begin to "identify disciplinary ideas associated with a compelling question." (D1.2.K-2)

## Dimension 2: Connections to Disciplinary Tools and Concepts

In Dimension 2, students will build on the compelling question, "What does liberty look like?" by working together to analyze one symbol of liberty: the American Flag. In the exercise below, students examine the symbolic parts of the flag and their meaning.

Teachers can begin this part of the lesson by asking students to use the following graphic organizer to facilitate their inquiry into the historical content related to the American Flag. There is great potential for students to organize their understanding of the symbolic components of the flag (a white star, a red stripe, a white stripe, or a blue field) and then demonstrate what they learned it symbolizes. For instance, if the student draws a superhero next to a red stripe the student now understands that the red stripe on the flag symbolizes strength and bravery.

| SYMBOL | MEANING |
|---|---|
| White Star | |
| Red Stripe | |
| White Stripe | |
| Blue Field | |

As students work through the graphic organizer, the teacher will want to help students with the following factual information regarding the flag's symbolism. To begin, it is important to note that on June 14, 1777, the Continental Congress passed the first Flag Act:

> Resolved that the flag of the United States be thirteen stripes, alternate red and white; that the union be thirteen stars, white in a blue field, representing a new Constellation.

The flag of the United States has gone through many incarnations as states have been added to the Union. At first, a stripe was added for every new state as well as a star but the basic design has stayed the same from the original flag with its circle of thirteen stars to our fifty-star flag of today. Below are some of the meanings of the flag:

- The thirteen stripes represent the original thirteen colonies.
- The number of stars on the flag represent the number of states in the Union.
- The stars on a blue field represent the creation of a new constellation.
- Red symbolizes Hardiness and Valor.
- White symbolizes Purity and Innocence.
- Blue symbolizes Vigilance, Perseverance, and Justice.

While working with students to initiate this process, the teacher can be selective with regards to essential, everyday words or those that are increasingly discipline-specific. For example, the following words help to describe symbols and discuss their connection to American history:

- Constellation
- Hardiness
- Valor
- Purity
- Innocence
- Vigilance
- Perseverance
- Justice

As students begin to connect these words with iconic American symbols, they will be investigating core democratic principles involving "equality, fairness, and respect" (D2. Civ.8.K–2), while working to acquire and evaluate the origin of these concepts as they pertain to the symbols that make up our national identity.

## Dimension 3: Evaluating Sources and Using Evidence

Once students have mastered the concept of symbols and how important they are, they can move towards more complicated and discipline-specific ideas, to obtain a better understanding of the question "What does liberty look like?" Students will work in groups to take a close look at the Statue of Liberty. In doing so, they "gather relevant information from one or two sources while using the origin and structure to guide the selection." (D3.1.K–2)

Begin this part of the lesson with an initial photograph of the Statue of Liberty.

Ask students to closely examine the image of the Statue of Liberty and answer the following questions: What sort of a statue is this? What is the statue doing? What are some interesting details that you see?

Then, show the students the four close-up views of the Statue of Liberty and discuss the information in the introduction. Pass out the Graphic Organizer: "The Statue of Liberty." Direct the students to draw one of the symbols of the statue (the tablet, crown, chains and/ or shackles, torch, or another illustration that shows a symbolic aspect of the statue). Then, with an illustration, key words, or even sentences, the student should identify and explain what the image symbolizes. (A graphic organizer for doing this, "The Statue of Liberty," is available online at: https://www.gilderlehrman.org/sites/default/files/inline-pdfs/Graphic%20 Organizer%20Statue.pdf)

For example, when the students are analyzing the Statue of Liberty they will discover many of our country's democratic values and principles embodied in the Statue's symbolism. The most obvious is Liberty's torch, held high to light the way out of the darkness and into the light of freedom. In fact, the statue's official name is "Liberty Enlightening the World." Another example are the broken shackles of tyranny around her feet as she strides forward. These are powerful symbols as well. Of course, the tablet she holds with the inscription "JULY IV MDCCLXXVI" honoring the founding of our nation

is another opportunity to discuss how our country came to be and the principles on which it was founded. For additional background information on the Statue of Liberty, see below:

The Statue of Liberty was a gift from the people of France to the people of the United States of America. Sculptor Frederic Auguste Bartholdi was asked to design the statue for America's 100th birthday in 1876. Problems with raising money for both the base of the statue as well as the statue itself set the project back ten years, but on October 28, 1886, the Statue of Liberty officially opened in New York harbor. Today it continues to greet travelers to New York and inspire all who look upon Lady Liberty.

The Statue of Liberty has an iron framework with a copper skin. That copper skin is only a little thicker than a penny. Even with such a thin skin, the statue weighs about 450,000 pounds. It rises 305.5 feet from the ground to the tip of the torch, and Lady Liberty herself is more than 111 feet tall from her feet to the top of her head. The Statue of Liberty, a symbol of Liberty itself, is also a combination of many other symbols:

- The tablet in her left hand is inscribed with "JULY IV MDCCLXXVI" (July 4, 1776) to recognize the creation of the United States of America.
- The seven rays on her crown represent the seven continents of the Earth.
- At her feet are broken chains and shackles to represent the throwing off of tyranny and oppression.
- The torch is a symbol of liberty. In fact, it is the source of the statue's official name: Liberty Enlightening the World.
- Lady Liberty is striding forward, symbolic of leading the way and lighting the path to Liberty and Freedom.

Teachers can access an additional exercise on the Great Seal of the United States via the Gilder Lehrman website: https://www.gilderlehrman.org/history-by-era/government-and-civics/resources/american-symbols-flag-statue-liberty-and-great-seal. In doing this assignment, students will have had experiences analyzing three American symbols (the American Flag, the Statue of Liberty, and the Great Seal of the United States) that help students understand the question *What does liberty look like?*

### Dimension 4: Communicating Conclusions and Taking Informed Action

This part of the lesson has two purposes: (1) To ensure that the students understand the purpose of symbolism and (2) To make sure that they can answer the compelling question, What does liberty look like?

First, students should be able to communicate their conclusion that the purpose of the symbolism they are studying is to communicate an idea through a visual image. It is visual shorthand, and it is not limited by language or reading ability. Next, reframe the compelling question "What does liberty look like?" by shifting it to "What is liberty in our classroom?" Expanding Dimension 1 of the lesson, remind students that liberty is the power to choose, think, and act for oneself, and it includes making choices that do what is best not only for oneself but for others as well. Ask students probing questions like:

- Does liberty mean doing whatever we want when we want in our classroom?

- What if what we want to do hurts others?
- What if what we want interferes with what someone else wants?
- Do we have classroom rules that promote liberty?
- Do we have classroom rules that inhibit liberty?
- How has your idea of liberty changed from our initial discussion?
- Does our understanding of the word change when we think of liberty in our classroom?

To demonstrate their understanding of liberty, have the students design a class symbol (e.g., flag, seal, statue). Have them discuss what symbols they would choose in creating a symbol for their own classroom. What colors should they choose, and what will those colors represent? What shapes or drawings should be on their symbol and what is their meaning? How does this symbol demonstrate an understanding of the value of liberty? This activity can be done as a whole group or in small groups with each group putting forward their design before one of the symbols is adopted as the class symbol. In this way, students are working to "present a summary of an argument using print, oral, and digital technologies." (D4.3.K–2.)

# Gilder Lehrman Institute of American History

Since its founding in 1994, the Gilder Lehrman Institute of American History has developed a solid foundation for providing a firsthand view of historic events and periods and content-rich resources to a national pool of elementary and secondary educators from public, parochial, private, and charter schools. Through Teacher Seminars, a 5,000+ Affiliate School Program, the Teaching Literacy through History program, Saturday Academies, access to leading historians, a collection of more than 60,000 original American history documents, and a website that received more than 2.6 million unique visitors in 2013, the Institute has earned an outstanding reputation as a nonprofit partner of schools and educators in preparing students for college readiness and future careers. For more Teaching Literacy through History lessons go to: http://gilderlehrman.org

*The author of this chapter is Tim Bailey, Director of Education at the Gilder Lehrman Institute, with contributions by David Riesenfeld, Master Teacher Fellow of the Gilder Lehrman Institute.*

# How Can You Make a Flag **Sing?**
## Investigating Stories in The Star-Spangled Banner

**National Museum of American History**

<table>
<tr><td colspan="3" align="center">HOW CAN YOU MAKE A FLAG SING?<br>Investigating Stories in the Star-Spangled Banner</td></tr>
<tr><td colspan="3" align="center">National Museum of American History (NMAH),<br>Office of Education and Public Engagement</td></tr>
<tr><td align="center">C3 Disciplinary Focus<br>U.S. History</td><td align="center">C3 Inquiry Focus<br>Evaluating sources and using evidence</td><td align="center">Content Topic<br>The War of 1812 and the Star-Spangled Banner</td></tr>
<tr><td colspan="3">

**C3 Focus Indicators**

**D1:** Explain how supporting questions help answer compelling questions in an inquiry (D1.4.3-5).

**D2:** Summarize how different kinds of historical sources are used to explain events in the past (D2.His.9.3-5).

**D3:** Use evidence to develop claims in response to compelling questions (D3.4.3-5).

**D4:** Construct explanations using reasoning, correct sequence, examples, and details with relevant information and data (D4.2.3-5).

</td></tr>
<tr><td align="center">Grade Level<br>3–5</td><td align="center">Resources<br>Resources cited in this chapter and educational resources on the NMAH website</td><td align="center">Time Required<br>1–2<br>class periods</td></tr>
</table>

# Introduction and Connections to the C3 Framework

As former Smithsonian curators Steven Lubar and Kathleen Kendrick explain in *Looking at Objects, Thinking About History,*[*] we should:

> [C]onsider each object with its many stories as holding diverse meanings for different people, past and present….What stories do the objects tell? What documents, and what stories from your history books, help you to understand what the objects meant to the people of the past? What can you say about the past by using objects?

When considering what constitutes a primary and a secondary source, and types of information that can be gleaned from primary sources, students may quickly think of documents such as letters, or even photographs. But where else should students look for

---

[*] Steven Lubar and Kathleen Kendrick, "Looking at Objects, Thinking about History," in "The Object of History: Behind the Scenes with the Curators of the National Museum of American History" at http://objectofhistory.org/guide/ (Roy Rosenzweig Center for History and New Media at George Mason University, Feb. 2007.) Web. Accessed in September 2014.

evidence about the past? What of societies and individuals that do not or cannot leave that sort of evidence behind?

Museum curators—the people who create the exhibitions and collect the objects in museums—study objects in order to understand history. Curators then use those objects to tell a story about the past. Because objects are the products of human workmanship—of human thought and effort—objects tell something about the people who designed, made, and used them. Like other primary sources, objects must be studied carefully and critically to assist curators and other historians in understanding the past. Objects naturally tie to the inquiry arc of the C3 Framework by inviting questioning, encouraging students to ponder the clues they provide, requiring an examination of supplemental materials, and modeling forms of expression and methods for taking action in the world.

In this lesson, students' job is to think about history through the lens of a museum curator, to read and interpret the Star-Spangled Banner, and to uncover its stories in order to make it "sing." The Star-Spangled Banner holds a variety of stories, from the story of its creator, Mary Pickersgill, an independent flagmaker; to the story of the Battle of Baltimore and its inspiration for our national anthem; to its life as a family treasure, a national symbol, and a museum object. Students can be given supporting documents from the Interactive Star-Spangled Banner website (http://amhistory.si.edu/starspangledbanner/) to accomplish their task of making the flag sing.

# Inquiry Arc

This lesson builds on the C3 Framework's emphasis on inquiry and historical literacies by guiding students through each dimension of the C3 inquiry arc. First, students build questioning skills in Dimension One by developing initial observation questions that build toward a compelling question. Next, students experience the work of historians by delving into supporting sources to build the tools of the discipline of history in Dimension Two. Students then learn to analyze these sources and evaluate evidence in Dimension Three. Finally, students express an interpretation in Dimension Four based on their analysis by developing either an exhibition label about one story of the banner or by selecting two supporting sources and developing an explanation of the story that connects them to the banner.

### Dimension 1: Developing Questions and Planning Inquiries

Dimension One of the C3 Framework focuses on questioning. Students should practice the questioning strategies that help curators to do their work. Questions such as, "Who made or used this object? What is the audience for this document? What is the value of this object for the people who made or used it?" are central to the work of curators as they assess the information provided by objects and other primary sources and begin to develop interpretations about the past using those sources. Students can be introduced to the observational and questioning practices of curators by being given an opportunity for simple observation. Learning to observe carefully is a crucial step in building the habits of mind to critically assess sources, including objects.

A View of the Bombardment of Fort McHenry, Print by J. Bower, Philadelphia, 1816.

DIVISION OF MILITARY HISTORY, NATIONAL MUSEUM OF AMERICAN HISTORY, SMITHSONIAN INSTITUTION

Have students observe the flag and make notes on their observations for 1–2 minutes. A resource that can be helpful is the interactive Star-Spangled Banner at http://amhistory. si.edu/starspangledbanner/interactive-flag.aspx, which highlights different parts of the banner. Ask them to share aloud what they observed or wondered about during their initial examination. Then, have students think of one or two more questions that they wonder about the flag and would like to investigate further. Sample questions might be:

- What is the object made from?
- Is it handmade or machine-made? How can we tell?
- When was it made?

Compile a class list of supporting questions to be addressed with the activity for Dimension Two. Alternatively, you may consider having students use the "Tips for Reading Objects" section of the Museum's "Engaging Students with Primary Sources" guide, which provides these and more suggested questions for interpreting historical sources of all kinds, including objects (see http://historyexplorer.si.edu/PrimarySources.pdf)

Ask students whether they think there is a single answer or a limited number of ways to answer the observational, supporting questions they developed. Explain that there are different kinds of questions: some are supporting questions, whose answers give us basic information about the object or time period such as the ones the class has just developed. Others are compelling questions that invite greater discussion or to which there might be multiple answers. By learning to ask supporting questions such as when it was made, or by whom, we are taking steps toward answering the larger compelling question about how you can make a flag "sing" and tell its stories. In this way, students are working toward a key indicator in Dimension One, to "explain how supporting questions help answer compelling questions in an inquiry." (D1.4.3-5)

# THE OBJECT OF HISTORY

It is important to note that objects can be used to discuss many different topics in history depending on how the object is used in an exhibition. As Lubar and Kendrick note, objects demonstrate connections among people and places, tell personal stories, and demonstrate moments in time or change over time. For further examples of the different stories in objects, see their essay on the website "The Object of History" at http://objectofhistory.org/guide/

**PRIMARY SOURCE**
**Object (or artifact):** An object in the historical sense is something that has been produced or shaped by human workmanship.

**Strengths:**
- Offer clues when no written documents exist
- Give clues to the materials that were available during the time period
- Create a visual record through three-dimensional facts: size, weight, texture
- Provide clues about function
- Convey information about everyday life
- Express ideas and information which either are not or cannot be shared effectively in writing or speech (forms, colors, effects of visual arts; personal fantasies, idioms of taste, unspoken significance, customs, and prejudices)

**Limitations:**
- Do not usually give clues to the who, what, where, why, when, how of an event
- Do not always provide clues as to their designer and/or owner
- Cannot tell us about the frequency of their use
- It is sometimes hard to tell the intended use of the object
- We cannot know from a single object:
  - how typical the object is of its time or of its type
  - whether there are parts missing
  - whether decoration is sparse or elaborate

## Dimension 2: Connections to Disciplinary Tools and Concepts

Dimension Two of the Framework focuses on knowledge development: how do objects help students to understand a given topic? In order for students to understand how a curator would present an object like the Star-Spangled Banner, they need to know something about its historical context.

Begin by introducing students to images of the Battle of Baltimore. (See one image on page 32; a further selection of such images is available on the Interactive Star-Spangled Banner website at http://amhistory.si.edu/starspangledbanner/baltimore-in-the-balance.aspx)

Have students observe the images and make observations about the information they see and read in these sources. Ask students what inferences they can draw about the time period, based on this information.

Next, explain to students that, like detectives or investigative journalists, curators were not witnesses to the event, but they weave together a story about the past by using clues offered by their "sources" and by asking good questions. In order to understand the events surrounding the flag, they, like curators, will use supporting sources to tell a story about the flag. Have students research the Battle of Baltimore in order to write a newspaper account about the event. (A sample activity of this kind, "Spreading the News," can be found at http://amhistory.si.edu/ourstory/pdf/starspangled/spreading_the_news.pdf.)

After completing their news stories, return to the students' list of supporting questions. How many of the questions were answered by the sources they found?

Then, explain that they will attempt to answer the remaining supporting questions, such as who created the flag. Provide students with sample sources related to the flag, including letters, personal accounts, or historians' interpretations. (An example of this is available in the activity "Historians are Detectives" at http://amhistory.si.edu/starspangledbanner/pdf/SSB_Historians_3_5.pdf). When students have completed the activity, review the sources they examined to answer their supporting questions. Create a chart that notes the type of source and the type of information the source provided. Emphasize that different kinds of sources provide different kinds of information, and that understanding this can help them to determine which kinds of sources will best answer the questions they develop.

The design of this set of activities is meant to build disciplinary literacy in history, while the content meets discipline-specific indicators in the C3 Framework, including the expectation that students will be able to "summarize how different kinds of historical sources are used to explain events in the past." (D2.His.9.3-5)

## Dimension 3: Evaluating Sources and Using Evidence

Museum curators must use disciplinary skills from history when developing exhibits. This part of the lesson emphasizes those disciplinary skills to help students deepen their knowledge about the War of 1812. The disciplinary skills of evaluating historical evidence that are developed in Dimension Two merge in this lesson with the skills developed in Dimension Three, which emphasizes analytical skills. When developing lessons using the C3 Framework, you may find an overlap between dimensions—that's expected! The dimensions build on one another but in that process of building, they overlap in places.

Following the guidelines of the C3 Framework, by fifth grade, students should be able to "use evidence to develop claims in response to compelling questions." (D3.4.3-5) When moving to developing analytical skills in Dimension Three, have students listen to a rendition of the Star-Spangled Banner. Next, have them carefully analyze the first stanza of the anthem. Although this text may be familiar, taking a careful look at the lyrics may help students to better understand the importance of considering perspective and audience when examining sources.

A variety of copies of the manuscript of the Star-Spangled Banner are available at: http://amhistory.si.edu/starspangledbanner/the-lyrics.aspx

Have students read the stanza in small groups or together as a class. Have students consider the meaning of the song in their own words by rewriting each phrase in their own words. Next, discuss the following contextual questions:

- What perspective might this author have on the battle?
- For whom might the author be writing?
- Who is the "we" in the text?
- What might this stanza say if written from someone on the opposing side of the battle?
- How might thinking about this source help us to more thoughtfully answer the compelling question?

Remind students that curators must carefully assess sources when building their interpretation of the past and when determining when and how to use particular sources in their exhibitions.

Explain next that they will return to looking at objects to help them return to the compelling question. When developing their initial set of supporting questions, many students may have asked about the missing pieces of the flag or the ragged edges. Show students the souvenir piece of the flag at http://amhistory.si.edu/starspangledbanner/family-keepsake.aspx.

Ask students to consider why someone would have wanted to take a piece of the banner, and what this suggests about the significance of the flag. Ask them if they have ever bought or collected a souvenir of a place they went to or that has meaning for them. People once collected pieces from the places they visited. The ordinary objects they collected as souvenirs reflected their wish to stay connected to the past. Explain that the Armistead family gave away dozens of small pieces of the flag. In fact, Georgiana Appleton, daughter of Lieutenant Colonel George Armistead, who was commander of Fort McHenry in 1814, wrote that "Indeed had we have given all we had been importuned for, little would be left to show." Then, have students read or read together the letter of December 1912 from Eben Appleton, the owner of the flag, presenting the flag to the Smithsonian, "where it could be conveniently seen by the public, and where it would be well cared for." Information about Appleton is available at http://amhistory.si.edu/starspangledbanner/national-treasure.aspx

The complete letter presenting the flag to the Smithsonian is accessible by clicking on images on that page or searching for "Appleton" in the website's search engine. Eben Appleton was Georgiana Appleton's son. In the letter, Appleton describes the circumstances in which Francis Scott Key, an eyewitness to the bombardment of Fort McHenry, wrote the lyrics of "The Star Spangled Banner." Be sure to source the document;

*O say, can you see,*
*by the dawn's early light,*

*What so proudly we hailed*
*at the twilight's last gleaming;*

*Whose broad stripes and bright stars*
*through the perilous fight,*

*O'er the ramparts we watched,*
*were so gallantly streaming?*

*And the rockets' red glare,*
*the bombs bursting in air,*

*Gave proof through the night*
*that our flag was still there,*

*O say, does that star–spangled*
*banner yet wave*

*O'er the land of the free,*
*and the home of the brave?*

that is, determine the author, date, and audience for the letter. You and the class can then discuss what the letter suggests about the history and meaning of the flag.

Dimension Three focuses on using evidence, and this activity is designed to train students in analyzing sources and in "us[ing] evidence to develop claims in response to compelling questions." (D3.4.3-5) As a conclusion to this phase of the lesson, ask students to consider how these pieces of evidence might help us to answer the compelling question: *How can you make a flag "sing"?*

### Dimension 4: Communicating Conclusions and Taking Informed Action

In Dimension Four, students are expected to "construct explanations using reasoning, correct sequence, examples, and details with relevant information and data." (D4.2.3-5) To practice these skills, have students return to the compelling question: How can you make a flag sing? Discuss the meaning of this question, which is that flags, like all objects, have stories to tell. Curators select objects carefully to help to tell a larger story. What story from the flag will your students tell? Have students select one story about the flag, then use the information and sources provided on the interactive Star-Spangled Banner website to write a paragraph summarizing the story of the flag as if they were creating an exhibition label. Students can examine the subsections of the Interactive Star-Spangled Banner website http://amhistory.si.edu/starspangledbanner/ to see samples of exhibition-style text.

Alternatively, students may select two objects from the supporting materials on the website to pair with the flag; you can then have them create an opening exhibition label that explains the relationship among all three objects. Students can also write their own explanation of what the flag means to them, and share their story along with an image on the online flag of the National Museum of American History at http://amhistory.si.edu/starspangledbanner/share-your-story.aspx

While much of the curator's job is to create exhibitions and to interpret the past, also essential to their work is the preservation of objects. Once students have taken on the role of curators in interpreting the stories of the Star-Spangled Banner, have them think about how they can be preservationists for their own objects. To explore issues of preservation, they can examine the effects of light on colored material, as well as other environmental factors that can damage historic textiles and other objects. (Two activities relating to these topics are available on the Museum's website: "Preservation and the Power of Light," accessible at http://amhistory.si.edu/ourstory/pdf/starspangled/preservation_and_light.pdf; and "The Museum Environment and Preservation," accessible at http://amhistory.si.edu/starspangledbanner/pdf/SSB_Museums_6_8.pdf ).

Dimension Four emphasizes that students should share their knowledge with others and take action based on that knowledge. Drawing on what students have learned about the flag's history, next have them discuss how and why the museum cares for the Star-Spangled Banner but also how individuals care for the American flag. Students can learn details about the Museum's preservation process at http://amhistory.si.edu/starspangledbanner/preservation-project.aspx, where they can also learn about practicing the proper care of the flag, including:

- Folding the flag: http://www.va.gov/opa/publications/celebrate/flagfold.pdf
- Disposing of the flag
- Carrying the flag

Information on these practices can be found in the American Flag Code: http://www.senate.gov/reference/resources/pdf/RL30243.pdf

Using this information, have students create an instructional video for their peers on caring for the flag, including a short summary of the history of the Star-Spangled Banner.

However, Dimension Four also teaches students to use their new knowledge to take action on issues in their world and communities. In order to "use a range of deliberative and democratic procedures to make decisions about and act on civic problems in their classrooms and schools," (D.4.8.3-5) next consider an important story in your local history. How is it being preserved? Are there historic sites that need maintenance? Are there organizations that need fundraising support to make local objects "sing"? Identify a promising project in your neighborhood, and have students brainstorm ways that they can help to preserve the story.

# About the Smithsonian's National Museum of American History

Through incomparable collections, rigorous research, and dynamic public outreach, the National Museum of American History explores the infinite richness and complexity of American history. We help people understand the past in order to make sense of the present and shape a more humane future.

The Museum serves over 5 million visitors to the building and receives nearly 3 million visits to its online education resources each year. Through its educational website, Smithsonian's History Explorer, and through webinars, webcasts, and in-person professional development, the Museum brings the rich primary source materials and dynamic strategies of the Smithsonian to the K–12 classroom.

The Museum is committed to sparking dialogue and debate through programs based on compelling questions. Such programs include the Museum's annual National Youth Summit, which brings together high school students, historians, and activists in a conversation about historical events and their lessons for contemporary life, and the Time Trials theater program that invites students to debate the legacy of a controversial figure in American history.

*The author of this chapter is Naomi Coquillon, Manager of Youth and Teacher Programs in the Office of Education and Public Engagement at the National Museum of American History. The copyright of this chapter is owned by Smithsonian/National Museum of American History. ©2014 Smithsonian/National Museum of American History. The Star-Spangled Banner on page 29 is in the Armed Forces History Collection, National Museum of American History, Smithsonian.*

# Is The **Necessary and Proper Clause** Really Necessary and Proper?

## *McCulloch v. Maryland* (1819)

**The Bill of Rights Institute**

The building of the Second Bank of the United States, Philadelphia, PA, whose constitutionality was the issue in *McCulloch v. Maryland*.
PHOTOGRAPH BY PETER CLERICUZIO

**Bill of Rights Institute, Education Department**

| C3 Disciplinary Focus | C3 Inquiry Focus | Content Topic |
|---|---|---|
| Civics, U.S. History | Developing questions and using evidence | Historic case relating to federal government powers |

**C3 Focus Indicators**

**D1:** Determine the kinds of sources that will be helpful in answering compelling and supporting questions, taking into consideration multiple points of view represented in the sources, the types of sources available, and the potential uses of the sources. (D1.5.9-12)

**D2:** Explain how the U.S. Constitution establishes a system of government that has powers, responsibilities, and limits that have changed over time and that are still contested. (D2.Civ.4.9-12)

**D3:** Identify evidence that draws information directly and substantively from multiple sources to detect inconsistencies in evidence in order to revise or strengthen claims. (D3.9-12)

**D3:** Develop claims and counterclaims while pointing out the strengths and limitations of both (D3.4.6-8).

**D4:** Construct explanations using sound reasoning, correct sequence (linear or non-linear), examples, and details with significant and pertinent information and data, while acknowledging the strengths and weaknesses of the explanation given its purpose (e.g., cause and effect, chronological, procedural, technical). (D4.2.9-12)

| Grade Level | Resources | Time Required |
|---|---|---|
| 9–12 | Resources cited in chapter; Bill of Rights Institute website | Two to three 45-minute class periods |

# Introduction and Connections to the C3 Framework

To what extent does the U. S. Constitution limit the powers of the federal government? In Article I, Section 8, Clauses 1-17 spell out specific powers of Congress. Clause 18 provides that

> The Congress shall have Power…To make all Laws which shall be necessary and proper for carrying into execution the foregoing powers, and all other Powers vested by this Constitution in the Government of the United States, or in any Department or Officer thereof.

Debate over the meaning of the Necessary and Proper Clause began at the Constitutional Convention of 1787 and continues to the present day. *Is the Necessary and Proper Clause really necessary and proper?* In order to pursue this question, one must consider the following:

- What did the phrase mean at the nation's founding?
- What constitutional principles are central to the debate?
- What has it meant at various times since then?
- What trends or patterns, if any, can be discerned in the ways the phrase has been understood through time?

Through this lesson, students will understand major events and controversies related to the interpretation of the Necessary and Proper Clause from the founding to the present day. They will understand and apply constitutional principles at issue in *McCulloch v. Maryland* (1819) to evaluate the Supreme Court's ruling in that case. Students will also develop a systematic approach to thinking through and applying the Constitution's provisions with respect to the powers of the U.S. government, as they engage in writing and civil discourse.

In a lesson designed for two or three 45-minute class periods, students will use historical sources to examine the issues and debates related to the Necessary and Proper Clause from 1787 to 1819. They will then show the enduring nature of the debate by identifying current events and controversies regarding the same constitutional principles. As students find examples of current events that raise questions regarding the extent of federal power, they will write summaries of the articles and then work in small groups to respond to the various questions framing this lesson.

You might extend the lesson to an additional two or three 45-minute class periods by examining debates surrounding the meaning of the Necessary and Proper Clause at specific times in history, such as the Jacksonian Era (1830s) and the 2010 Supreme Court decision, *United States v. Comstock*.

# Inquiry Arc

### Dimension 1: Developing Questions and Planning Inquiries

This inquiry is focused on the compelling question: Is the Necessary and Proper Clause really necessary and proper? In this part of the lesson, students will determine the kinds of sources that will be useful in the inquiry. (D1.5.9-12) At the same time, it is important for students to see the value in the compelling question, so you should spend a few minutes making the case for why this compelling question, and the supporting questions, matter. The following supporting questions might be provided to students, or you could work with students to develop their own supporting questions.

- What are the powers enumerated to the federal government in Article 1 Section 8 Clauses 1-17?

- What are some hypothetical examples of "necessary and proper" actions by federal government that might be suggested, but are not stated, in order to carry out the powers that are specifically listed in Article 1 Section 8 Clauses 1-17?

- What are some examples of times when the Necessary and Proper Clause was called into use?

- What were the facts in the case and the major implications for the Supreme Court decision in *McCulloch v. Maryland*?

Begin this activity with some familiar concepts from everyday life, and lead students in a brief discussion about applications of the Necessary and Proper Clause. Provide students with an overview of Article 1 of the U.S. Constitution as background. Follow this background work with a brief discussion about the role of government in regulating some of the following things while explaining connections to the Constitution.

- Light bulbs
- Speed limits
- Health insurance
- Education standards
- Consumer safety regulations

This discussion will help students understand the nature and importance of the compelling question and begin to brainstorm ways to find out the meaning of the Necessary and Proper Clause.

After this opening activity, which could be completed in a little as 20 minutes, the focus shifts to D.1.5.9-12 as students determine useful sources. Generate a list of trustworthy sources for students to consider. The list should include, but not necessarily be limited to:

- The Constitution itself
- The Federalist Papers
- Anti-Federalist writings
- Public and private writings of the Founders
- Court decisions
- Scholarly commentary

Have students describe why the sources might be useful, attending to the viewpoints represented in the sources and the potential information within. Students should make sure that they have included sources that are representative of all potential viewpoints and that the sources provide direct access to information that will be relevant for their inquiry. This will likely require considerable support. Such support might go so far as providing students with a narrow list of sources and even excerpts.

The scope of federal government power under the Constitution has been a major point of controversy since the beginning of the Republic. During the Revolutionary War, the United States government accumulated significant debt, but each state used a different form of currency. Washington's Secretary of the Treasury, Alexander Hamilton, advocated the creation of the First Bank of the United States in order to handle the war debt, create a standard form of currency, and encourage the establishment of a prosperous commercial republic. This was the start of a longstanding argument between those who argue that freedom and prosperity are best promoted by political decentralization and those who believe that a powerful central government is needed to ensure progress and prevent state governments from undermining the national interest. The Necessary and Proper Clause gives Congress the power to "make all Laws which shall be necessary and proper for carrying into Execution the foregoing Powers, and all other Powers vested by this Constitution in the Government of the United States." It is not a free-standing grant of power, but rather was intended to give Congress the power to enact laws needed to "carry into execution" the various powers granted to the federal government by other parts of the Constitution. Congress drafted a twenty-year charter for the Bank in 1791. President Washington sought advice regarding its constitutionality and then signed the bill.

Congress did not renew the Bank's charter when it expired in 1811. However, following the War of 1812 and its associated debt, Congress established the Second Bank of the U.S. in 1816. Once again, those who supported a National Bank maintained that it was necessary to control the amount of unregulated paper money, such as banknotes issued by state-chartered banks. However, most states opposed branches of the National Bank within their borders. They did not want the National Bank competing with their own banks, and objected to the establishment of a National Bank as an unconstitutional exercise of Congress's power. The state of Maryland imposed a tax on the bank of $15,000/year, which cashier James McCulloch of the Baltimore branch refused to pay. The issue of the constitutionality of the Bank reached the Supreme Court in 1819. Maryland argued that as a sovereign state, it had the power to tax any business within its borders. McCulloch's attorneys argued that it was "necessary and proper" for Congress to establish a national bank in order to carry out its enumerated powers.

In the Court's unanimous opinion, Chief Justice John Marshall wrote, "Although, among the enumerated powers of government, we do not find the word 'bank,'…we find the great powers to lay and collect taxes; to borrow money; to regulate commerce…Let

the end be legitimate, let it be within the scope of the constitution, and all means which are appropriate, which are plainly adapted to that end, which are not prohibited, but consist with the letter and spirit of the constitution, are constitutional." The Supreme Court had endorsed Hamilton's interpretation of "necessary."

Further, the Court ruled that Maryland could not tax the national bank: "the power to tax involves the power to destroy. . . If the states may tax one instrument, employed by the [federal] government in the execution of its powers, they may tax any and every other instrument…This was not intended by the American people. They did not design to make their government dependent on the states."

Marshall also noted an important difference between the Constitution and the Articles of Confederation. The Articles said that the states retained all powers not "expressly" given to the federal government. The Tenth Amendment, Marshall noted, did not include the word "expressly." This was further evidence, he argued, that the Constitution did not limit Congress to doing only those things specifically listed in Article I. Creation of a bank was an implied power of Congress. In this landmark decision, Marshall invoked the Commerce Clause, the Necessary and Proper Clause, and the Supremacy Clause.

However, Marshall noted that his reasoning was not a blank check for assertions of federal power. The Necessary and Proper Clause, he wrote, authorized only such laws as promote "legitimate" ends that are "within the scope of the constitution," and use "means which are appropriate, which are plainly adapted to that end, which are not prohibited, but consist with the letter and spirit of the constitution." The proper scope of the federal government's authority continues to be a subject of serious debate.

John Marshall.
STEEL ENGRAVING, 1861, BY ALONZO CHAPPEL, NATIONAL PORTRAIT GALLERY

## Dimension 2: Connections to Disciplinary Tools and Concepts

Once students have done some initial source work, the focus should shift to the establishment of essential shared knowledge among students about the Necessary and Proper Clause. With this work, students will be able to develop knowledge described in D2.Civ.4.9-12 about the "establishment of a system of government that has powers, responsibilities, and limits that have changed over time that and are still contested." To accomplish this task, you might provide direct instruction to lead students as they explore the four supporting questions.

- What are the powers enumerated to the federal government in Article 1 Section 8 Clauses 1-17?
- What are some hypothetical examples of "necessary and proper" actions by federal government that might be suggested, but are not stated, in order to carry out the powers that are specifically listed in Article 1 Section 8 Clauses 1-17?
- What are some examples of times when the Necessary and Proper Clause was called into use?
- What were the facts in the case and the major implications for the Supreme Court decision in *McCulloch v. Maryland?*

Students will work in four small groups using available texts and technology, with each group focusing on one of the supporting questions. In each group, students will develop responses to the group's assigned question.

Next, lead a whole class discussion in which groups report their responses, filling in an outline to summarize the students' work.

## Dimension 3: Evaluating Sources and Using Evidence

At this point in the inquiry, students should begin to analyze relevant sources to locate information that will help them respond to the compelling questions. Careful consideration should be given to the actual task (extracting information) and to how you might support the work. To support students, build on the work done at the beginning of the lesson where students determined the types of sources that might be useful. Now it's time to use those sources to make claims. Specific sources are recommended here, but you will have to make some decisions about what to use in the classroom. Page 45 includes an example of a chart that can support students as they draw information from the sources. As students practice working with sources in this way they are building up the skills described in D3.3.9-12 where they "identify evidence that draws information directly and substantively" from sources as they make claims in response to the compelling question.

Students will work individually and in groups, using the following historical sources in order to support the claims they will make. These sources are available in the Bill of Rights Institute Resource: *McCulloch v. Maryland* lesson, Supreme Court DBQs Vol. 2, in the Resources section of the Bill of Rights Institute website, http://www.billofrightsinstitute.org.

- United States Constitution, Article I, Section 8, Clause 18
- Letter from An Old Whig, 1787
- *Brutus No. 1,* 1787
- *Federalist No. 33,* 1788
- *Federalist No. 39,* 1788
- Thomas Jefferson, Opinion on the Constitutionality of the Bill for Establishing a National Bank, 1791
- Memorandum No. 1, Edmund Randolph to George Washington, 1791
- Alexander Hamilton's Opinion on the National Bank, 1791
- *McCulloch v. Maryland* Unanimous Decision, 1819
- President Andrew Jackson's Veto Message, 1832
- King Andrew the First Cartoon, 1833
- *U.S. v. Comstock* Majority Opinion, 2010
- *U.S. v. Comstock* Dissent, 2010

The following kind of chart can be used to support students as they draw out evidence from these sources.

| Source Title | Summary of Source | Relevant Information | Relevant Claim |
|---|---|---|---|
|  |  |  |  |
|  |  |  |  |
|  |  |  |  |
|  |  |  |  |

## Dimension 4: Communicating Conclusions and Taking Informed Action

As a concluding activity, students write a paragraph describing their findings. This paragraph will consist of high level claims in response to the compelling question and evidence that supports those claims. This paragraph will not be the final product, so students should just focus on getting their claims and evidence down on paper. The emphasis in this part of the lesson is on students adapting their claims for presentation in a debate. (D4.2.9-12)

To culminate the inquiry, students will participate in a fishbowl debate using this resolution:

**Resolved:** The Necessary and Proper Clause is not necessary or proper because it makes the principles of federalism and limited government obsolete.

1. Divide the class into two groups.
2. Assign one group to be the affirmative side and the other to be the negative side.
3. Give students a few minutes prep time and have each side choose the first two or three students who will speak.
4. Place two "hot seats" in the center of the room, between the two groups.
5. Have each side's first speaker take the hot seat.
6. Using civil discourse, reasoned arguments, and citing their sources, these students make each side's opening argument. Students respond directly to one another, targeting the specific argument being made by their opponent in the hot seat.
7. After a brief designated period of time, give the signal for the next speaker from each side to take the hot seats. Students take care not to simply repeat points that have previously been made, but to extend and build on the initial arguments with relevant new facts and evidence. Students may volunteer to speak after the first few speakers have provided the framework of the debate.
8. Proceed in this manner until all useful arguments for each side have been presented and most students have been speakers.

Through the inquiry activities suggested in this analysis of *McCulloch v. Maryland*, students will develop the skills to engage in some of the most central debates running through the history of the republic: What necessary and proper powers have the people delegated to their central government, and what powers remain with the states and the people themselves? In what ways do modern expectations and conceptions of government reflect or challenge the conceptions of the Founders? What kind of government is best able to protect the people's rights, provide for their safety, and promote their happiness? As they grapple with such important questions, students cultivate the skills needed to participate in reasoned debate and to take informed action as competent citizens.

# About the Bill of Rights Institute

Established in 1999, the Bill of Rights Institute is a 501(c)(3) not for profit charity focused on providing educational resources on America's Founding documents and principles for teachers and students of American History and Civics.

Its mission is to educate young people about the words and ideas of America's Founders, the liberties guaranteed in our Founding documents, and how our Founding principles continue to affect and shape a free society. It is the goal of the Institute to help the next generation understand the freedom and opportunity the Constitution offers.

The vision of the Institute is to create a citizenry that has the knowledge, values, dispositions, and skills to exercise the rights and responsibilities needed to maintain a free society.

*The author of this chapter is Gennie Westbrook, Director of Curriculum and Professional Development at the Bill of Rights Institute.*

# CHAPTER 5

# How Are Productivity and Standards of Living Impacted by **Technology?**

**The Center for Economic Education and Entrepreneurship, University of Delaware**

Apple barrels wait to be loaded onto barges on the Erie Canal in this historical postcard, ca. 1870.
COURTESY ERIE CANAL MUSEUM, HTTP://WWW.ERIECANALMUSEUM.ORG

# Introduction and Connections to the C3 Framework

In the discipline of economics, students learn the economic way of thinking, which is a reasoning process that considers costs as well as benefits when making a decision. To do this, students must use the tools of cost/benefit analysis, make an analysis of supply and demand, and consider the future consequences that may result from the decision. Using these analytical tools and following the C3 Framework's Inquiry Arc, middle school students can learn how technological change has driven economic change since human history began.

Technology increases productivity—that is, the amount of output per unit of input. Increased productivity means more of the goods and services that increase peoples' standards of living. These increases result not just from the change in technology, but also from increases in the education and skill level of the work force. This lesson focuses on the impact of technology.

Technological change has resulted in increased productivity and hence higher standards of living ever since humans began using tools. Historically, adaptation to technological innovation occurs over long periods of time; however, the rate of that change has been accelerating, and citizens' responses to those innovations do not always keep pace with the changes.

Although changes can take a long time, benefits have generally accrued not only to the producers but also to other workers and society as a whole. For example, one of the unintended consequences of Gutenberg's printing press was the democratization and dissemination of information, which led to upheavals in Europe in the relationships between the ordinary citizen, the government, and the Catholic Church. Printed communication also spread changes in how to produce goods and services leading to the Industrial Revolution.

Forward to the 21st century. Information technology has allowed everyone, including some of the poorest and most isolated people on the planet, instantaneous access to current events. People also now have the ability to see how other cultures and nations live, resulting in a desire to increase their own standard of living from subsistence-level food production to a higher standard of living. As technology increases productivity, costs of production fall, which means that a worker's income has more purchasing power. Therefore, people's standards of living tend to rise. Hans Rosling's four-minute video, 200 Countries, 200 Years, traces how countries' standards of living have increased as technological change has accelerated (see http://www.gapminder.org). But these benefits come with costs.

One of the major costs related to technological change is that of job destruction. Sometimes termed "creative destruction," this process leaves many individual workers scrambling to make a living with skills that have or may become obsolete through technological innovation or from increased competition from workers around the world, both skilled and unskilled. At the same time, many new jobs are created. Our students must develop skills that promote lifelong learning and which allow them to adapt to the changes in technology that are necessary for future careers, and to improve the quality of their lives.

# Inquiry Arc

### Dimension 1: Developing Questions and Planning Inquiries

If you ask middle school students how technology, productivity, and standards of living are related, they most likely will find the question unexciting and fail to see the importance of searching for an answer unless they see a connection to their own lives.

Use the smart phone to generate interest in technology and its impact. Pose the following questions. How many of you use smart phones? How does the use of smart phones affect your lives or activities in which you participate? How would your life change if smart phones didn't exist? Have smart phones made people more productive? If so, in what way? Explain that a technological change is a new way of doing something or is manifested in a product that does things differently. Point out that a smart phone is an example of a technological change and one that certainly has affected their lives.

Following this discussion, inform students that they are going to analyze different technologies to answer this compelling question: *How are productivity and standards of living impacted by technology?*

The C3 Framework suggests that students should be able to "explain how a question represents key ideas in the field." (D1.1.6-8) The compelling question framing this lesson focuses on the key idea of the effect of technology on productivity and standards of living. Lead students in a discussion about this key idea. You can structure this discussion around these prompts.

- What is an example of a technology that has changed your life?
- What are some technologies that you have learned about in history that helped improve economies?
- What are some modern technologies that are making lives better for people in less developed countries?

The discussion could go in a lot of directions. Some students may argue that smart phones in fact make them less productive rather than more so. Teachers may be inclined to agree! But there are clear examples where this is not the case. In developing countries, for example, online banking via smart phone has revolutionized the livelihoods of many people who do not have access to good roads. Students might argue that throughout history, technological change has impacted people's standards of living and quality of life. The construction of the Erie Canal, which most students study sometime during their middle school experience, demonstrates the links between technology, productivity, and standards of living over time. Inform students that they are going to explore the answer to the compelling question by first using economic analysis to study the impact of the construction of the Erie Canal and then applying this economic way of thinking to a technological change of their choice.

To answer the compelling question, students will need to apply an economic way of thinking using cost/benefit analysis. Additionally, you might extend the lesson to have students examine supply and demand, assess future consequences, and make connections among events and developments in broader historical contexts. This can be accomplished through chronologically viewing the productivity changes caused by the technological innovations.

With your support, students can inquire about the compelling question and deepen their understanding of the economic impact of technology. To guide the students in their research, use these supporting questions, which can be utilized when studying any technological change:

- How did this technology affect productivity?
- How did this technology affect standards of living?
- How did this technology affect the quality of life?

## Dimension 2: Connections to Disciplinary Tools and Concepts

The C3 Framework says that students should be able to "explain why standards of living increase as productivity improves." (D2.Eco.13.6-8) One way to support students as they develop such knowledge is to provide historical examples related to the concept. One of the most important economic tools for analyzing the effect of a technological change is a cost/benefit analysis. Using the authoritative sources (see our list of sources at the end of this chapter), have groups of students identify the costs and benefits (or the losers and gainers) of the construction of the Erie Canal—from before the canal was built through later expansions and other technological innovations.



From their research, students can organize their findings into a cost/benefit chart. See the sample Erie Canal Cost/Benefit Analysis Chart below (Figure 1). This cost/benefit analysis leads students to see how shipping on the canal changed life from Buffalo to Albany to New York City and to the Western territories.

**Figure 1** Erie Canal Cost/Benefit Analysis Chart

| TECHNOLOGY: CANALS | |
|---|---|
| **Costs** (What was given up?) | **Benefits** (What gains were made?) |
| High cost of construction | Faster way to move goods |
| Take a lot of time to build | Lower costs of shipping |
| Tax increases | Lower prices for products |
| Competition is greater | Wider variety of manufactured goods |
| Job losses if jobs are not near the canal Loss of income for owners of mules and horses over time | Increased jobs—canal construction, for western farmers, bargemen, barge construction, steam powered tugboats, merchants in cities |
| Increased prices for goods in the interior parts of NY not near the canal | More produce/grains for cities in the East |

The next tool that students can use to analyze the effects of technology on standards of living is supply and demand analysis. Staying with our Erie Canal example, assign students a specific good that was shipped on the canal (i.e., wheat, corn, lumber, minerals, clothing, dishes, manufactured goods) or the resources that were used in the shipping process (tools, barges, steam engines, "hoggees," who were workers that guided the mules, stables for the mules, harnesses). Using this data, students can construct a supply and demand graph. The graph below (Figure 2), shows the prices, supply and demand for flour before and after the construction of the Erie Canal. The graph demonstrates that the decrease in the cost of production increased supply. This in turn decreased the prices of the goods, both agricultural and manufactured. The net effect was that workers and consumers had more money to spend on goods and services, which increased their standard of living. Similar supply and demand analyses can be applied when examining the impact of any technological change, which reinforces the relationship between productivity and standard of living. From supply and demand analysis, students should conclude that every technological change results in an increase in productivity which in turn increases supply leading to lower prices of goods and services. Lower prices increase consumers' purchasing power, making them better off.

Supply/demand graphs can be scary, but there is no need to panic. Remember that when supply increases (i.e. increase in productivity), we can make more stuff (Q) for a lower price (P). On the other hand, if supply decreases, as in the case of wars or natural disasters, we produce less stuff and prices increase. Middle school students can comprehend this concept with your help.

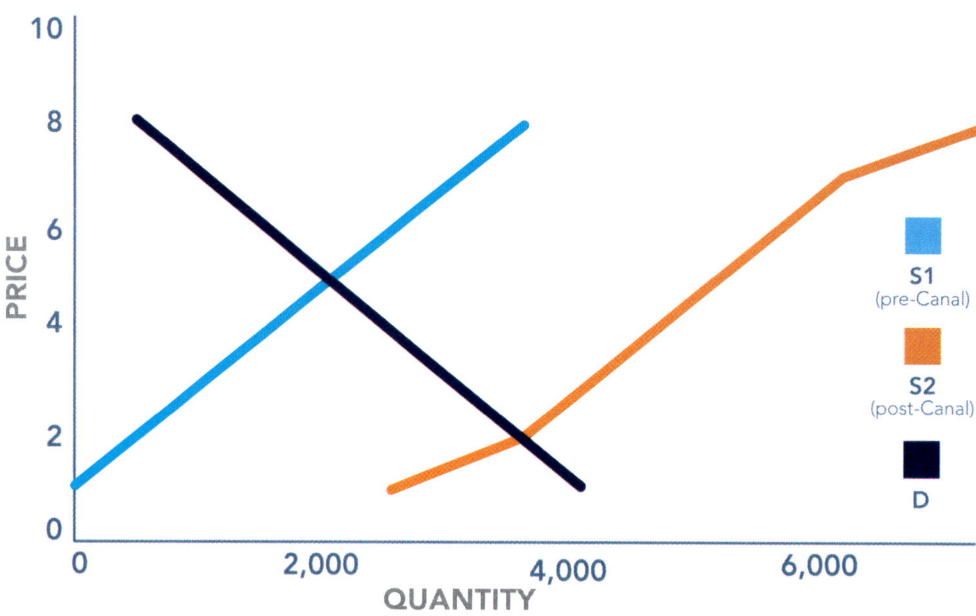

**Figure 2** Supply and Demand for Flour on the Erie Canal



The information for Figure 2 is taken from Scott Derks and Tony Smith, *The Value of a Dollar: Colonial Era to the Civil War, 1600-1865* (Grey House Publishing, 2005).

# Dimension 3: Evaluating Sources and Using Evidence

Dimension 3 of the C3 Framework sets forth an expectation that students will construct arguments and explanations emerging from their inquiries, using information from sources as evidence. (D3.3.6-8) Underlying this search for evidence is the application of the economic way of thinking. Remind students that their analysis of the construction of the Erie Canal gave them the opportunity to learn about the economic way of thinking in an historical context.

Now, have students select another technological change and use the economic way of thinking to address the compelling and supporting questions.

**COMPELLING QUESTION**
- How are productivity and standards of living impacted by technology?

**SUPPORTING QUESTIONS**
- How do specific technologies affect productivity?
- How do specific technologies affect standards of living?
- How do specific technologies affect the quality of life?

Examples of technological change are numerous and can be a bit overwhelming for students. To scaffold the process, provide students with a list of technologies that they can examine using the same approaches described in the section on Dimension 2.

- Automobiles
- Internet
- Pony Express
- Radio and Television
- Refrigeration
- Telegraph
- Transcontinental Railroad
- Telephone
- Washing machine

Support students as they locate relevant information (see the sources at the end of this chapter) regarding the costs and benefits of their assigned technology. Students should complete the blank cost/benefits chart for their technology. If students are working in groups or pairs, make sure you convene the groups as a whole class so they can share their findings. The collective findings, for all nine technologies, will be useful as students begin to synthesize their findings in response to the compelling question.

# Dimension 4: Communicating Conclusions and Taking Informed Action

For this lesson, the explanations and arguments that students construct focus on the relationship between standards of living and productivity, given technological change.

A response to the compelling question in this lesson is highly dependent on the supporting questions about the costs and benefits of technological change. The C3 Framework suggests that developing explanations in response to supporting questions is key to a successful inquiry. (D4.2.6-8) The supporting questions included in this chapter were stipulated to frame students' investigation of specific technologies.

Students should compose a response to each of these supporting questions for their assigned technology. As they share responses, students should begin to synthesize ideas toward developing a response to the compelling question.

Students can share findings with their peers through PowerPoint slides, a news article, visuals, posters, and short videos. Regardless of the method chosen, each presentation should include the answers to the supporting questions above and ultimately the compelling question. Student presentations should make the case on why their technology had the greatest impact on productivity, standard of living, and quality of life.

## Sources

### ERIE CANAL
- http://www.eriecanal.org under the historical documents
- http://www.canals.ny.gov/history/history.html
- http://xroads.virginia.edu/~MA02/volpe/canal/history_body.html (On the history of canal politics)
- http://www.uh.edu/engines/epi1420.htm (This episode gives numbers on how the canal reduced the time and thus the costs of shipping goods from Albany to Buffalo, then down the Hudson to New York harbor.)
- http://www.canals.org/researchers/Canal_Profiles/United_States/Northeast/Erie_Canal
- http://www.lerner.udel.edu/centers/ceee. See under Resources.

### PONY EXPRESS
- http://www.nps.gov/poex/historyculture/index.htm
- http://ponyexpress.org/history/
- http://www.sfmuseum.org/hist1/pxpress.html

### TELEGRAPH
- http://www.americaslibrary.gov/jb/civil/jb_civil_telegrap_2.html
- http://www.history.com/topics/telegraph

### TRANSCONTINENTAL RAILROAD
- http://www.uh.edu/engines/epi2844.htm
- http://www.archives.gov/exhibits/treasures_of_congress/text/page15_text.html
- http://www.americaslibrary.gov/jb/civil/jb_civil_telegrap_2.html
- http://www.pbs.org/weta/thewest/program/episodes/five/index.htm
- http://www.pbs.org/weta/thewest/resources/archives/five/railact.htm

### TELEPHONE
- http://www.uh.edu/engines/epi1487.htm
- http://www.uh.edu/engines/epi1098.htm
- http://www.uh.edu/engines/epi748.htm
- http://www.learnnc.org/lp/editions/nchist-newcentury/5092

### RADIO AND TELEVISION
- http://www.history.com/topics/radio-and-television
- http://www.uh.edu/engines/epi1681.htm
- http://www.uh.edu/engines/epi1649.htm

### AUTOMOBILES
- http://www.uh.edu/engines/epi1596.htm
- http://www.uh.edu/engines/epi2402.htm
- http://www.uh.edu/engines/epi2520.htm
- http://www.uh.edu/engines/epi2560.htm
- http://www.history.com/topics/model-t
- http://l3d.cs.colorado.edu/systems/agentsheets/New-Vista/automobile/

### REFRIGERATION
- http://www.history-magazine.com/refrig.html
- http://goarticles.com/article/History-and-Impact-of-Refrigeration-on-Society/5627038/
- http://www.uh.edu/engines/ashrae.htm (democratization of comfort)

### INTERNET
- http://www.history.com/topics/invention-of-the-internet
- http://www.uh.edu/engines/epi2117.htm
- http://www.ideafinder.com/history/inventions/internet.htm
- http://www.uh.edu/engines/epi2798.htm
- http://www.uh.edu/engines/epi675.htm

### WASHING MACHINE
- http://www.ted.com/talks/hans_rosling_and_the_magic_washing_machine.html
- http://www.smh.com.au/federal-politics/society-and-culture/how-the-washing-machine-changed-the-world-20120407-1wi1k.html

# About the University of Delaware's Center for Economic Education and Entrepreneurship

The University of Delaware's Center for Economic Education and Entrepreneurship (CEEE) provides opportunities for professional development, develops dynamic teacher resources, and produces engaging student programming statewide. CEEE's primary goal is to ensure that economics, personal finance, and entrepreneurship are integrated into the K–12 core curriculum to prepare Delaware students to make informed decisions in today's global economy.

*The authors of this chapter are Bonnie Meszaros, Associate Director, and Barbara Emery, Program Coordinator, of the University of Delaware's Center for Economic Education and Entrepreneurship.*

# What Did **I Get Myself Into**?

## Guiding Students Through The National History Day Process

**National History Day**

A presentation by students during the group performance category at the Kenneth E. Behring National History Day Contest.

NATIONAL HISTORY DAY

**National History Day**

| **C3 Disciplinary Focus**<br>History | **C3 Inquiry Focus**<br>Using evidence from multiple sources to construct an argument | **Content Topic**<br>U.S. or World History |
|---|---|---|

**C3 Focus Indicators**

**D1:** Explain how a question represents key ideas in the field. (D1.1.6-8)

**D1:** Explain how a question reflects an enduring issue in the field. (D1.1.9-12)

**D2:** Use questions generated about individuals and groups to analyze why they, and the developments they shaped, are seen as historically significant. (D2.His.3.6-8)

**D2:** Use questions generated about individuals and groups to assess how the significance of their actions changes over time and is shaped by the historical context. (D2.His.3.9-12)

**D3:** Gather relevant information from multiple sources while using the origin, authority, structure, context, and corroborative value of the sources to guide the selection. (D3.1.6-8)

**D3:** Gather relevant information from multiple sources representing a wide range of views while using the origin, authority, structure, context, and corroborative value of the sources to guide the selection. (D3.1.9-12)

**D3:** Evaluate the credibility of a source by determining its relevance and intended use. (D3.2.6-8)

**D3:** Evaluate the credibility of a source by examining how experts value the source. (D3.2.9-12)

**D4:** Present adaptations of arguments and explanations on topics of interest to others to reach audiences and venues outside the classroom using print and oral technologies (e.g., posters, essays, letters, debates, speeches, reports, and maps) and digital technologies (e.g., Internet, social media, and digital documentary). (D4.3.6-8)

**D4:** Present adaptations of arguments and explanations that feature evocative ideas and perspectives on issues and topics to reach a range of audiences and venues outside the classroom using print and oral technologies (e.g., posters, essays, letters, debates, speeches, reports, and maps) and digital technologies (e.g., Internet, social media, and digital documentary). (D4.3.9-12)

| **Grade Level**<br>6–12 | **Resources**<br>vary by project type | **Time Required**<br>4 lessons |
|---|---|---|

# Introduction and Connections to the C3 Framework

Students in schools are often told what they will learn. They are told what books to read, what questions to answer, and what step comes next. National History Day (NHD) allows students to shift gears. Rather than being a passenger in the learning experience, students have the opportunity to become the driver. By giving students agency, teachers unlock the potential of students in ways that no teacher-created assignment ever could. This chapter gets to the heart of some of the common problems faced by teachers pursuing an inquiry-based approach to learning using the model of an NHD project.

The C3 Framework is designed around an inquiry arc: the idea that students should ask questions, be given the tools to dive into those questions, and then, ultimately have an opportunity to answer the questions in a meaningful context.

# Inquiry Arc

The hardest part of many projects is getting started. We have all stood in front of a messy closet, sighed, and closed the door. For many students, starting an inquiry-based research project is the same feeling—it is overwhelming, and easier to close the door and ignore it for as long as possible. Once students have the opportunity to develop a topic that is of reasonable scope and sequence, fits the parameters established by the teacher, and, most importantly, piques his or her interest, then the process of inquiry can begin.

A good research question should connect to the interest of the students. Accessing students' interests will make them more engaged and willing to work much harder than when a project is assigned. In addition, the question needs to be manageable in scope. It is impossible to propose a research question about large swaths of history (e.g., World War II, the Russian Revolution, Ancient Rome), but often it is possible to use these areas of interest as a starting point to help students develop questions that are manageable.

**Dimension 1:** Developing Questions and Planning Inquiries

**D1.1.6-8.** Explain how a question represents key ideas in the field.
**D1.1.9-12.** Explain how a question reflects an enduring issue in the field.

For the inquiry process to begin, teachers need to help guide students to develop a strong question that will set them on the path to plan a successful inquiry. When students are given latitude to choose their own topic (with the parameters and guidelines established by the teacher), several common issues appear.

**"I don't know what I want to do. Can't you just pick something for me?"**

For some students, this is a lot of choice—sometimes too much. It can become overwhelming, and some will shut down and want the teacher to do it for them. One strategy to help this student is to have him or her tell you what they DO NOT want to study.

**FIGURE 1**

| I WOULD LIKE TO STUDY…. |
| --- |
| Governments, laws, and who is in control |
| How militaries operate |
| How people worship and express religious beliefs |
| How women and other groups earned equal rights in society |
| The growth of cities |
| The history of a particular group of people within a larger society |
| How ideas develop in society |
| The story of my family's roots |
| How people lived |
| How money impacts peoples' lives |
| Art, culture, music, sports, and other forms of entertainment |
| What happens when large groups of people move from one part of the world to another |
| The development of the rural parts of a nation |
| The way that workers operate |
| How ordinary people live |
| How governments develop and change over time |

Start by giving students a list of broad topic areas such as political history or public history. You can then introduce more specific descriptions of topic areas (Figure 1) based on the age and ability of the students in your class.

If you learn that the student is interested in family history, the development of cities, and the impact of the physical world, then maybe you can suggest the 1666 Great London Fire, San Francisco's 1906 earthquake, or the 1883 eruption of Krakatoa as a starting point. Similarly, a student with an interest in sports and rights and responsibilities might be interested in the case of Curt Flood, or of Jackie Robinson's Court Martial for refusing to sit at the back of the bus. Offer suggestions based on interests, but allow students to explore and decide independently.

➡️ **"I have so many interests. I think the Progressives are cool, but I really like the American Revolution and have always wanted to do a project on Ancient Greece. Help!"**

The opposite of your first challenge is the challenge that some students have lots of interests and have trouble narrowing them down (or change them frequently). In this case, you need to help put limits. Often, these students will have a stronger interest in an aspect of history (military, social, cultural) than a time period. If you can get to the heart of that, then sometimes that can help you in directing them.

**FIGURE 2**

| WHEN STUDENTS GET "STUCK," HERE ARE A FEW TIPS | | |
|---|---|---|
| Toss out some ideas for the students to consider. This should be a back-and-forth process. You might want to redirect students to think about a different aspect of a topic. | Make students curious. For example, ask, "Have you ever heard of Grace Murray Hopper?" Say, "She was cool; check her out," and then walk away. Drop ideas, but leave it up to the students to seize the idea or walk away from it. | Bring in a local resource. This could be a guest speaker from a local library, regional or affiliate NHD coordinator, or a local historical society. This speaker could offer the students suggestions, either about local history connections or topics where resources are available locally. |

Sometimes interests come from popular culture. Books, movies, and television shows are great starting points to pique a student's interest. But ask them "what about that book/movie/TV show caught your interest?" Make sure that the interest goes beyond a particular actor or story plot.

➡️ **"Can't I just use George Washington for my topic? He should be easy."**

Ah, the common topic. One year when I was introducing the theme of "The Individual in History," I gave the students a list of over 200 leaders to start considering. When I asked them for five names they might consider studying (the names could come from on or off the list) about 25% of the class put Walt Disney on their list. Why did they do that? Because he was familiar and seemed "fun." I told the class that unless they could come up with a unique or interesting "twist" on Disney, he was off their list. One group did, and the others moved onto other topics. One group even found an alternative topic, studying the propaganda cartoons made by Warner Brothers during World War II.

Once students get interested in a topic, they should consider limiting and refining their topic so that they can plan an effective inquiry. Here is where a teacher sets the parameters. Some teachers might choose to give students choices, while others place limits on their choices based on the curriculum (e.g., students must choose a U.S. history topic, or students must choose a topic based on Europe in the twentieth century).

## Dimension 2: Connections to Disciplinary Tools and Concepts

Now that students have their topics at least nominally established, here is where inquiry really takes off. The most substantial component of the process is research and building the background knowledge needed to make an argument. Here is where students become historians. Often that process begins with tertiary sources—reading about the topic in a textbook or encyclopedia article—and then progresses to secondary and primary sources. Before they can write a thesis statement or make an argument, they need to build a knowledge base.

For students to be sure that their topic is feasible, they need to engage in basic research. Take the students to the library and have them find at least one primary and one secondary source that apply to their topic. Depending on the age and level of the course, introductory lessons or library orientations may or may not be necessary. Assess the needs of your class and plan accordingly.

Generally road bumps in this section of the research process tend to fall into one of two categories:

➡️ **"I can't find ANYTHING on my topic."**

This complaint generally is the result of general laziness or a sign that a student's topic is too narrow and needs to be broadened. For laziness, I would often challenge the student. One student came to me one day and said, "I just can't find a copy of the Marshall Plan." My first response was to ask him, "so where did you look?" and I got the typical response of "everywhere—it's impossible to find primary sources on this one." Rather than resorting to Google, I took the student to the history reference section of the library and said, "Are there any sets of books here that look even remotely helpful?" He did gaze to a set of older books called the *Annals of America*, which were sorted by time period. I encouraged him to use the table of contents, and magically, found documents on the Marshall Plan. Do not accept "there's nothing" until you prove the students wrong. Then tell them that you do not want to hear whining until they exhaust all of their sources. It rarely happens twice.

➡️ **"There is so much on my topic, I don't know where to start."**

Here is your opposite problem. Often it is because a student has chosen a topic that is too broad ("Remember when I told you that all of D-Day is way too big a topic for this project?"). Help the student narrow down his or her focus from all of D-Day to the role that a particular leader or group played in the invasion.

Sometimes the problem is not the topic, but rather the student's ability to organize information. These are key skills that students need to be taught. Students need to take some time to process their information. They need to have a method of taking notes. This can be using pens and notecards, or this could be using electronic versions.

Students need help sorting their facts into logical buckets (such as context, background, the event, impacts of the event). Students also need to be able to identify their "top docs," with the best quotes, pictures, and multimedia clips.

Some ways to help students:

- Create and maintain a set of really good research links. Make sure students are directed to places like the Library of Congress, the National Archives, and legitimate, vetted, online sources (if not, we all know where they will go…).
- Add good research sites (like "Chronicling America") and good university-based archives sites (like Dickinson College's "House Divided").
- Add to these links. Encourage students to share good finds with you and add them to an electronically accessible list for all.
- Get ideas for links from other teachers' sites or from the NHD site (http://www.nhd.org). No need to start from scratch.

➡️ **"You expect me to make an annotated bibliography? I don't even know what that is."**

An annotated bibliography is as much a tool for an NHD judge as it is for an NHD researcher. The key to this is to build it as you go. Students should be entering sources as they find them, even if their annotations are not complete. A good annotated bibliography helps students visualize the breadth and depth of their research.

Teachers should encourage students to turn in new sources in small manageable chunks. Each student turns in one source. Offer feedback and return it to the student. Then require for the next deadline that they show corrections to their first entry and add two more. This allows you to help solve small problems (i.e., confusion over whether a document is primary or secondary) before they become large problems, and it helps to see gaps in a student's research ("so you think you want to do a documentary, but I don't see any images or video in this bibliography yet. Work on that next week during our research time.")

Some tips for supporting students as they develop their understanding of the significance of the historical topics they are investigating:

- Have students locate (or provide students with) differing perspectives on the person, event, or idea they are investigating. Students will probably need to use secondary sources or textbooks.
- If students are working in groups, have each student make her or his own judgment about the significance of the person, event, or idea and then bring the students together to debate their differences of opinion.

## Dimension 3: Evaluating Sources and Using Evidence

➡ **"You said we had to find the source, not that we had to read it."**

Once students gather and organize their sources, many of them think that their research is done. When you ask them, "have you actually read the sources?" you often see averted glances and smiles. I always called this phase of the process Research Analysis. Here students need to be able to sort and organize the sources they have, find the diamonds, and throw out the trash. Before they can do that, they often have to spend some time looking at their documents.

Both the Library of Congress (http://www.loc.gov/teachers/usingprimarysources/guides. html) and the National Archives (http://www.archives.gov/education/lessons/worksheets/) offer great primary source analysis tools that can be used to help students break down and analyze their sources. Use these tools (or make your own) and model the process with students. It is probably not feasible to break down every single primary source this way, but each student should go through this process with his or her best sources. This can be very helpful because weak sources rarely get very far on these organizers.

You know your students better than anyone, and it is your job to set the bar for those students. Teacher discretion is key—while it would be common for a sixth grader to start with (and maybe even cite) an encyclopedia entry, I would not allow an honors junior in high school to do the same. You set the bar as to what sources are acceptable or not for your students. Maybe you require a certain reading level of books, but can make allowances for students who are English Language Learners or have learning disabilities. Maybe you put an overall limit (no more than three encyclopedia-type sources).

➡ **"What's my best source? Well, all of them!"**

Next, students need to find their diamonds. These are the best quotes, images, or video clips, the ones that their project cannot live without and become the central focus of a panel on an exhibit board, a turning point in a documentary, or evidentiary claim in a paper. Have students identify their three diamonds and bring them to class one day.

Have the students give an elevator pitch as to HOW this document helps them answer their thesis. Sometimes you find that students are missing something key in this process ("how can you look at the Louisiana Purchase and not have a map"?) or ("how can you have primary source video footage of Elizabeth I? There were no cameras, so I'm guessing that documentary clip is a secondary source….").

➡ **"But I found it…can't I just keep it in my annotated bibliography?"**

Once students have things organized, they need to take out the trash. Students need to acknowledge what did not help them. Many students are resistant to doing this, especially if they have already put it in a bibliography. But it is important to know as a researcher that sometimes you need to toss what does not work to focus on what does.

## Dimension 4: Communicating Conclusions and Taking Informed Action

➡ **"Relax…it's not due for another month!"**

When it comes to project creation, the first, second, and most important challenge students face is procrastination (it's that closet thing again…). This is where as a teacher you need to make procrastination impossible. Regular checkpoints where students need to show measurable progress is key. Some ways to make that happen:

Require a storyboard/outline and a plan. Critique and then require that it be edited. Make sure students are not creating bad projects.

Require the project in phases. Have checkpoints where students are required to workshop their process papers, show a friend a clip from their documentary, or edit their papers. Are the exhibit boards too big to bring back and forth to school? Not a problem. Tell students to snap a picture with their cell phone and send it to you. Project the picture in front of the class and critique.

Beware of the kitchen sink phenomenon (also very common in short answer questions). Sometimes students think that the best way to show their knowledge is to cram in every fact that they know and, like putting dirty dishes in the sink, finish the project. These projects tend to be messy and, just like the dishes in the sink, are not clean. Here is where you need to help students wash the dishes, move them out of the way, and selectively edit.

Reinforce over and over again the need for revision. The C3 Framework stresses that teachers should give students opportunities to adapt arguments and explanations. (D4.3.9-12) The most successful NHD students are those who edit their projects with teacher feedback, regional judge feedback, and feedback from the state or affiliate level. Sometimes students find from one level to another that they need to "start clean" or redesign a segment of a documentary, revise the conclusion of a performance, re-write a paper's introduction, or change out multimedia options on a documentary.

# About National History Day

National History Day (NHD) is a dynamic curriculum program for students in grades 6-12. Students choose historical topics related to a theme and conduct extensive research. After analyzing and interpreting their sources and drawing conclusions, students present their work in original papers, websites, exhibits, performances, and documentaries. NHD sponsors workshops for students and teachers and identifies and celebrates outstanding Social Studies educators across the nation. NHD works with educators to develop curriculum materials to support the innovative teaching of NHD in classrooms. Recent materials include "U.S. History in Global Perspective", "Teaching the Civil War in the 21st Century," and an online collaborative World War I primary teaching resource. More information can be found at http://www.nhd.org.

*The author of this chapter is Lynne O'Hara, Director of Programs at National History Day.*

# What's The **Question?**
## Inquiry With The National Archives DocsTeach

**The National Archives and Records Administration**

The National Archives, Washington, D.C.
PHOTOGRAPH BY DAVID SAMUEL

**National Archives and Records Administration,
Education and Public Programs Division**

| C3 Disciplinary Focus<br>U.S. History | C3 Inquiry Focus<br>Evaluating primary sources and communicating conclusions | Content Topic<br>U.S. Primary Sources |
| --- | --- | --- |

**C3 Focus Indicators**

**D1:** Determine the kinds of sources that will be helpful in answering compelling and supporting questions, taking into consideration multiple points of views represented in the sources. (D1.5.6-8)

**D1:** Determine the kinds of sources that will be helpful in answering compelling and supporting questions, taking into consideration multiple points of view represented in the sources, the types of sources available, and the potential uses of the sources. (D1.5.9-12)

**D2:** Use other historical sources to infer a plausible maker, date, place of origin, and intended audience for historical sources where this information is not easily identified. (D2.His.11.6-8)

**D2:** Critique the usefulness of historical sources for a specific historical inquiry based on their maker, date, place of origin, intended audience, and purpose. (D2.His.11.9-12)

**D3:** Identify evidence that draws information from multiple sources to support claims, noting evidentiary limitations. (D3.3.6-8)

**D3:** Identify evidence that draws information directly and substantively from multiple sources to detect inconsistencies in evidence in order to revise or strengthen claims. (D3.3.9-12)

**D4:** Present adaptations of arguments and explanations on topics of interest to others to reach audiences and venues outside the classroom using print and oral technologies (e.g., posters, essays, letters, debates, speeches, reports, and maps) and digital technologies (e.g., Internet, social media, and digital documentary). (D4.3.6-8)

**D4:** Present adaptations of arguments and explanations that feature evocative ideas and perspectives on issues and topics to reach a range of audiences and venues outside the classroom using print and oral technologies (e.g., posters, essays, letters, debates, speeches, reports, and maps) and digital technologies (e.g., Internet, social media, and digital documentary). (D4.3.9-12)

| Grade Level<br>6–12 | Resources<br>Resources cited in this chapter; DocsTeach and other resources on the National Archives website | Time Required<br>Variable |
| --- | --- | --- |

# Introduction and Connections to the C3 Framework

Inquiry is at the heart of the C3 Framework and the National Archives' mission. If you are one of the millions of people who have visited the National Archives in Washington, DC to see the Declaration of Independence, Constitution and the Bill of Rights, you might have noticed a cart outside our entrance with the sign "Ask the Question." Every day, archivists around the country get questions from people trying to uncover the past. Heck, our general email address, the one when a researcher doesn't exactly specify whom to contact, is inquire@nara.gov.

Likewise, the C3 Framework's Inquiry Arc opens with questions. This focus on questions reflects the ethos of the National Archives and is suggestive of the nature of the disciplines that make up social studies.

It is our educational mission to help teachers, students and the public to find and make sense of these documents to uncover the past. Researching and analyzing documents from institutions like the National Archives is the cornerstone of the discipline of history. By exposing students to a wide range of perspectives and a variety of document types (written, photographs, posters, etc) available in our holdings, students learn the tools of the trade for historians.

Students examine digital copies of National Archives documents.
EZRA GREGG

This chapter focuses on using primary sources from the National Archives and our educational resource, DocsTeach, to help students conduct inquiries about events in U.S. history. In this chapter, we highlight four areas of historical content to illustrate how the DocsTeach resource can support inquiry—The drafting of the U.S. Constitution; 1970s America; Food conservation efforts during World War I; and the effectiveness of the Freedman's Bureau. This chapter also offers suggestions for using the four dimensions of the Inquiry Arc to examine a featured nineteenth-century document relating to immigration restrictions (pp. 72–73).

# Inquiry Arc

**Dimension 1:** Developing Questions and Planning Inquiries

Dimension 1 of the C3 Framework focuses on developing questions, and DocsTeach (http://www.docsteach.org), which offers access to over 7,500 primary source documents, can help jumpstart the inquiry process. Teachers can use DocsTeach to create activities that focus on important content in social studies and to build prior knowledge and activate a student's interest in the area of study. Students can use DocsTeach to search for documents to help generate compelling questions.



## DOCSTEACH

DocsTeach is a place to browse or search to uncover thousands of primary source documents (http://docsteach.org/documents) about a wide variety of topics. It is also a place to both find and create interactive educational activities (http://docsteach.org/activities) that use these documents. At DocsTeach, educators can modify and personalize any activity to meet the specific needs of their classroom. Educators can also create their own interactive lesson from scratch and share it with their students.

At DocsTeach, educational activities can be created using seven interactive tools (http://docsteach.org/tools)—Finding a Sequence, Focusing on the Details, Making Connections, Mapping History, Seeing the Big Picture, Weighing the Evidence, and Interpreting Data. The National Archives created these templates to help educators incorporate primary source documents into their classrooms and teach students historical thinking skills at the same time.

A Guide to Creating Your DocsTeach Activity is available on our Education Updates blog at http://www.archives.gov/education/pdf/GuidetoCreatingYourDocsTeachActivity.pdf (this URL is case-sensitive). This step-by-step guide walks you through the process of creating your own activity from start to finish. In addition, there are short tutorials about creating DocsTeach activities using each of these interactive tools on National Archives YouTube channel at http://www.youtube.com/course?list=EC118B3DEBEBA03192.

The "Focusing on Details" activity creation tool (http://docsteach.org/tools/focusing-on-details) is particularly suited for initiating the inquiry process. This tool can be used to focus attention on intriguing sources to quickly engage students and spark inquiries into a broader topic. After selecting a compelling document to analyze, this tool also allows you to include discussion questions and even modify the full document to spur analysis. Teachers can modify the original source by putting a spotlight on a particular key phrase, zooming in or cropping out a particular aspect, or blacking out certain features to focus analysis. If working with two documents, this tool also allows students to compare and contrast the pair.

Compelling and supporting questions are not created in a vacuum. Primary sources can act as a catalyst for students' development of questions while also helping teachers preload some disciplinary content into the process.

For example, two versions of the Preamble to the US Constitution—one from early August 1789 from the first printed draft of the Constitution and the other the final ratified version in mid-September 1789—can provide an interesting opportunity to open an inquiry about the dynamic nature of the founder's views on the government. In a related DocsTeach activity (http://docsteach.org/activities/68), students are asked to explain the differences between these versions, and their significance, as well as how the change reflected the founder's changing views. This short 10-minute activity can jump start an inquiry into the purposes of government.

Another way to prompt students to create compelling questions on their own is have them explore the collection of documents that are available in DocsTeach (http://docsteach.org/documents). Representing a tiny percentage of the billions of documents in our holdings, the 7,500+ documents available here can be used to spur further research.

At DocsTeach, students can browse different historical eras or search for specific topics. They can filter their searches by era and types of sources as well. In addition, for certain topics, there is a growing selection of themed pages. At the page for 1970s America (http://docsteach.org/home/70s), documents are grouped in topics relevant to this time period. The Environment, Women's Rights, and Watergate are a few found in 1970s America.

Just a quick exploration of these sources can provide just as many compelling and supporting questions as answers. For example when looking at photographs under

"Women's Rights" students may ask: Why would Betty Ford support the ERA? What is the ERA? Why are women dressed in 'crazy' costumes holding signs? All of these are potential supporting questions in an inquiry. The teacher can demonstrate how each of these questions may relate to a larger compelling question such as "What can be done when constitutionally guaranteed rights are not enjoyed equally by Americans?"

## Dimension 2: Connections to Disciplinary Tools and Concepts

In the age of Google and smartphones, it's easy to find information, but much harder to slow down, stop, and critically analyze the information right in front of you. Historians seek answers to their questions about the past by practicing active thinking during the search process. They seek evidence in a variety of materials. They use the work of other scholars found in the form of secondary sources and tap into primary historical sources created at the time of the event in a variety of formats. They put on the brakes and carefully study all aspects of a document; the seen and unseen. Then they contextualize and corroborate the document with others they located and determine the relevance and utility of this document in relationship to their historical question.

This process is second-nature for historians. To help your students develop these analytical skills, you can use a set of steps for careful document analysis. The following steps found on DocsTeach (http://docsteach.org/resources) can be used for any type of document (written document, photograph, map, chart, audio/movie clip).

1.  **Before getting into the content of the document, look at it in a very general sense and ask basic questions.** Consider the document's type: "What kind of document are we looking at?" For example, for textual documents, is it a newspaper, letter, report? For artifacts, what material is this made of? For video, is it a propaganda film, cartoon, or training video?

2.  **Find unique characteristics of the document** (which will vary depending on document type). Note any markings or special qualities. These characteristics will help students understand the document in context. For example: Are there any symbols, letterhead, handwritten versus typed text, stamps, seals, or notations? Is there a background, color, or tone? Are there facial expressions in photographs, or other telling features? Is there narration or special effects? Is there a key?

3.  **Attempt to identify the creator and the content of the document.** Break down the document by asking "Who, What, Where, When, Why and How?"

4.  **Rephrase the document into plain language.** Students should determine the content of the document and speculate for whom and why it was created. Help students understand the document in historical context.

By working through these steps, students can develop the C3 skills mentioned in D2.His.11.6-8. These skills provide a foundation for evaluating the relevancy and utility

CONTINUED ON PAGE 74

# Petition from the North American Turner-Bund (Gymnastic Union) Opposing Immigration Restriction, February 22, 1890

http://docsteach.org/documents/7452138/detail

## Developing Questions and Planning Inquiries

Teachers can model the process of developing questions for inquiries by providing students with National Archives documents such as the "Petition from the North American Turner-Bund (Gymnastic Union) Opposing Immigration Restriction" featured here. This document raises issues related to a compelling question "Why has/does the United States limit immigrants that enter the United States?" or "Should the United States limit the number of immigrants that enter the United States? Why or why not?"

Whether this compelling question is provided or student generated, an intriguing primary source document can help students generate supporting questions and begin considering sources for their inquiry. These new supporting questions can drive the Inquiry Arc as students must search for answers.

A cursory examination of this document may make students wonder about which law is being referred to by the petitioners (the 1891 Immigration Act that established tighter standards for potential immigrants and stronger Federal control over immigration), what the North American Turner-Bund is (a German-American cultural and gymnastic society that was founded in 1848 by German immigrants), and which document the writers quote to compare the current Congress with British tyrants ("He has endeavored to prevent the population of these states..." is from the list of grievances in the Declaration of Independence). They may also be curious about contemporary opinions about immigration in the late 19th century, when there was beginning to be a shift in the nationalities entering the United States—with sizable numbers of immigrants arriving from Southern and Eastern Europe for the first time.

## Connections to Disciplinary Tools and Approach

Thorough document analysis is important when working with a primary source in order for it to become evidence in one's inquiry. Understanding the historical context in which a document was created, paying attention to various perspectives, and evaluating the role of cause and effect surrounding a document are equally important. When working with a primary source, we must both look within and beyond the confines of the document to search for answers.

Working within this source, students should closely examine the document itself.

- Who created this document?
- When was this document created?
- Why do you think this document was created?
- What arguments does the petition make for not changing the immigration and naturalization laws? What is the validity of these arguments?
- What does this document tell you about the time period it was written?

End your class's analysis of this document by asking students what additional supporting questions are left unanswered and/or are generated through the process. These questions will drive students into researching beyond what the document itself can answer in order to understand the broader historical context in which this document was created.

Students will be drawn to exploring resources that illustrate the reactions and challenges related to the mass immigration in the late 19th and early 20th centuries. They can investigate topics such as the Chinese Exclusion Act, the Alien Contract Labor laws, and late 19th century Immigration Acts, as well as subsequent events such as the Red Scare and the Immigration Quota Acts of 1921 and 1924.

## Evaluating Sources and Using Evidence

After students have located additional primary and secondary sources to answer their supporting and compelling questions, teachers should help guide their students through the process of evaluating and corroborating the sources. In this process, students will start to gather evidence from these multiple sources and begin to develop claims about their topic of inquiry.

The use of additional sources will clarify observations made in the initial analysis by students of the petition to Congress, and will allow for new insights and understanding as they grapple with questions such as: Why was Congress considering changing its immigration policy in the late 19th century? What were opinions and attitudes towards immigration to the United States in the late 19th century? What was the effect of petitions such as this on the legislative process?

## Communicating Conclusions and Taking Informed Action

Students will then use the evidence sparked from their initial analysis and subsequent investigation to create explanations, arguments, or creative adaptations (e.g., speeches, or documentaries). Students can take informed action by drawing what they learned through analysis and research into the civic sphere, and connecting the historical topic of immigration to current events.

In this example, encourage students to take what they have learned about the Federal Government's past approaches to immigration and summarize that information in a letter to their U.S. Senator or Representative about the current issue of unaccompanied minors seeking entrance into the United States as immigrants. Students could follow the model of the featured petition, gather signatures to show support for their opinion on this issue, and send their petitions to their U.S. Senators or Representatives, or post their petitions to http://petitions.whitehouse.gov and build awareness for the campaign via social media.

# NORTH-AMERICAN TURNER-BUND (GYMNASTIC UNION.)

## OFFICE NATIONAL EXECUTIVE COMMITTEE.

St. Louis, Mo., February 22d, 1890.

*To the Hon. Senate and House of Representatives of the United States:*

The "North-American Turner-Bund" (Gymnastic Union), an organization, comprising some 40,000 citizens of this country, both native and naturalized, does hereby respectfully, but most earnestly, protest against the passage of any and all of the measures, now before your honorable body, designed to materially change the present national laws on immigration and naturalization.

As some of the reasons (among many) for our protest we mention the following:

*First.* These proposed measures are fraught with the same mischief and breathe the same spirit which caused the founders of this Republic to rise in rebellion against a British tyrant, and to hurl at him the following indictment:

"He has endeavored to prevent the population of these States; for that purpose obstructing the laws for naturalization of foreigners; refusing to pass others to encourage their migration hither, and raising the conditions of new appropriations of lands."

All such legislation is therefore directly opposed to the very spirit of our institutions, and cannot be defended upon any mere plea of expediency or self-interest.

*Second.* The industry, thrift and honest intelligence of the immigrant has, for more than a hundred years past, been a chief factor in developing the mineral, agricultural, commercial and industrial resources of this country, and in raising it to its present proud position among the nations of the World.

There is room in this broad land for many millions more of human beings. By maintaining the liberal policy of our forefathers who extended to every new-comer the warm hand of welcome we may and will continue to multiply our national wealth and the comforts and happiness of our people. By surrounding ourselves with a Chinese wall of intolerance we will as surely invite stagnation and retrogression.

*Third.* The patriotic devotion of those who have in the last century emigrated to our land and acquired a right of citizenship among us, has been such as to win a proud place in its history, and not least among them are the members of our own organization. What right have we to assume that the character of those to come under a continued liberal policy of immigration will be one particle lower than of those who came before? In truth, the very proposal of these illiberal measures is an affront to the bearer of every non-English name, no matter how long the line of his ancestry that helped to build up this nation!

*Fourth.* Any material change of our present naturalization laws, looking to the discouragement of naturalization, must be regarded as uncalled-for and mischievous. Not merely should we encourage those who have cast their fortunes among us to soon become loyal members of our body-politic, but the very existence of large bodies of unnaturalized residents would seem to constitute a menace to our institutions. Love of a free country can best be bred in men by securing to them the full and early enjoyment of its privileges and blessings.

*Fifth.* The scheme proposed, of emigrant-inquisition through our consular and governmental representatives abroad, is impracticable and unjust. It will aid the wicked merely, and deter the good. No European government will assist in retaining its bad elements and in forwarding the desirable. Besides, a system of espionage, like this, is odious and degrading to all concerned.

*Sixth.* Our existing laws, if rigidly and justly enforced, afford ample protection against all undesirable and criminal immigration; but no such system of laws, as now proposed, can be enacted without violating the fundamental principles of our National Compact and darkening the brightest pages of our National history.

In the sentiments of this protest the mighty host of men who sought this land for the freedom and enlightment which it promised, we feel assured, will heartily join. They must regret, as they will resent, the apparent spirit of race-prejudice and nativism which these proposed laws so liberally display, and for them all, as well as the members of our own particular organization, we do most earnestly petition you not to lend your voice and vote to their enactment.

Very Respectfully,

The National Executive Committee of the North-American Turner-Bund.

Hugo Muench, President.
John Toensfeldt, Vice-President.
J. Rudolf Bollinger, Cor. Secretary.
Dr. Wm. Drechsler, Rec. Secretary.
Richard Boesewetter, Treasurer.
Richard Bartholdt,
Ernst Helfensteller,
Jacob Von Gerichten,
Albert H. Haeseler.

**We, the undersigned, respectfully join the above petition.**

of a historical source based on information such as maker, date, place of origin, intended audience, and purpose. Building students' document analysis skills and speculating or perhaps even determining why a source was created and for whom, along with understanding its historical context, takes practice and reinforcement.

Activities within DocsTeach can develop these skills. For example while studying World War I, the activity "Comparing World War I Posters Urging Americans to Conserve Food for the War Effort" (http://docsteach.org/activities/4876) encourages students to theorize why the U.S. Food Administration created posters in different languages, and then determine what techniques were used to appeal to citizens based on a close analysis of the posters.

## Dimension 3: Evaluating Sources and Using Evidence

"Because I said so!"

"Because the source says so!"

"Because the source says so I believe that!"

This sequence reflects the increasing sophistication we want students to develop when using historical sources. Tools from the National Archives can assist students with the process of becoming more sophisticated in the use of evidence in their inquiries.

Teachers can use the DocsTeach.org tool, "Weighing the Evidence," to help students learn how to evaluate sources to build an argument with primary sources. "Weighing the Evidence" (http://docsteach.org/tools/weighing-the-evidence) asks students to analyze, interpret and evaluate documents to determine their credibility and the validity of their evidence towards a specific historical conclusion. Students are presented with a series of primary sources and a scale that has opposing interpretations on either side. Depending

---

**MORE ONLINE DOCUMENTS**

While students can spend quite a bit of time gathering primary sources on just DocsTeach alone, the 7,000 documents available there represent just the tip of the iceberg of the records of the National Archives. Millions of digital copies of documents are available in our Online Catalog (OPA) (http://www.archives.gov/research/search). In addition, OPA describes the vast majority of our records that have yet to be digitized. And students can always email an archivist with their research question at inquire@nara.gov.

As students can search for documents, they should consider how the compelling and supporting questions they are exploring are related to the Federal government—knowing this will help students find more answers to their question. Was a law passed by Congress related to the event? Did it occur during someone's Presidency? Was there a court case related to the issue? Does a federal agency oversee a related aspect? The more answers a student has to these questions, the better prepared they will be to find materials in the National Archives. In addition, if students know the creator and purpose of a document, they may have a better sense of its perspectives on an issue and its relevance to their topic.

on their analysis of the document and how much they feel it supports a particular interpretation, they can place it on the scale closer to the appropriate interpretation. At the conclusion of the activity, students are asked to explain their interpretations.

For example, in the activity "How Effective were the Efforts of the Freedmen's Bureau?" (http://docsteach.org/activities/28) students evaluate the effectiveness of the Freedmen's Bureau in assisting formerly enslaved persons by analyzing documents. Upon being freed, the formerly enslaved persons faced many challenges. What did former enslaved persons need once slavery ended? What did they want after being freed? What resources did they have to meet needs and wants? In this activity, students consider these questions by arranging seven different documents—including a land certificate, a register of marriages, a set of teachers' rules, and a photograph of a rations line—on the scale according to the extent to which they think the document supports their interpretation of the issue of the effectiveness of the Freedmen's Bureau in providing for the wants and needs of formerly enslaved persons. After the sources have been arranged on the scale, you can lead a discussion about students' decisions. A discussion of this sort can help students clarify and articulate their reasoning before trying to use information from the source as evidence in an argument.



## Dimension 4: Communicating Conclusions and Taking Informed Action

Skills developed through primary source analysis and DocsTeach pave the way for students to craft and share historical essays, documentaries, museum-style exhibits, or other alternative products emerging from their discoveries and conclusions.

Several of the activity creation tools in DocsTeach can assist students in writing explanations and arguments. The "Weighing the Evidence" tool can be used as a pre-writing tool for students constructing arguments. After completing the activity, students can share their thoughts with their teacher via email by clicking "I'm Done" and typing up to a 2,000 character response. After completing further research, students can then create an argument citing specific evidence that they gathered from these historical sources and other resources. In much the same way, DocsTeach's "Finding a Sequence" (http://docsteach.org/tools/finding-a-sequence) and "Making Connections" (http://docsteach.org/tools/making-connections) tools can aid students in constructing explanations of a historical process.

To help students communicate conclusions as suggested in the C3 Framework, you can also share samples of public history. Historical articles from the National Archives magazine Prologue (http://www.archives.gov/publications/prologue/) can inspire and guide students in crafting historical stories. The footnotes used in the articles, as well as

the publication, Citing Records in the National Archives of the United States (http://www.
archives.gov/publications/general-info-leaflets/17-citing-records.html) provide samples for
students creating bibliographies and footnotes. Online exhibits, such as the "Records of
Rights," (http://www.archives.gov/exhibits/) highlight how museum curators at the National
Archives approach creating a virtual exhibition with National Archives documents.

# About the National Archives and Records Administration

The National Archives and Records Administration is an independent Federal agency
that preserves and shares with the public the records that trace the story of our nation,
government, and the American people. The National Archives holds over 12 billion
records in 44 locations across the country. Of all documents and materials created in the
course of business conducted by the United States Federal government, only 1%–5% are so
important for legal or historical reasons that they are kept by us forever.

As the nation's record keeper, it is our mission to preserve and provide access to the
documents of the Federal Government. We help the public find documents to uncover
evidence to support their research. Our billions of records created by Congress, the
President, the Courts, and hundreds of federal agencies illuminate countless historical
topics.

The National Archives Education and Public Programs team is dedicated to ensuring our
nation's documents are available and accessible to teachers and students.

*The authors of this chapter are Kris Maldre Jarosik and Christopher Zarr, who are education
specialists at the Education and Public Programs Division of the National Archives and
Records Administration.*

# Why Did The Suffragists Choose **Public Protest** Tactics?

**The Library of Congress**

Official program – Woman suffrage procession, Washington, D.C. March 3, 1913.
LIBRARY OF CONGRESS, HTTP://WWW.LOC.GOV/RESOURCE/PPMSCA.12512

| Library of Congress Educational Outreach Division | | |
| --- | --- | --- |
| **C3 Disciplinary Focus**<br>U.S. History, Civics | **C3 Inquiry Focus**<br>Developing Questions and Evaluating Primary Sources | **Content Topic**<br>The Women's Suffrage Movement |

**C3 Focus Indicators**

**D1:** Determine the kinds of sources that will be helpful in answering compelling and supporting questions, taking into consideration the different opinions people have about how to answer the questions. (D1.5.3-5)

**D2:** Use information about a historical source, including the maker, date, place of origin, intended audience, and purpose to judge the extent to which the source is useful for studying a particular topic. (D2.His.13.3-5)

**D3:** Gather relevant information from multiple sources while using the origin, structure, and context to guide the selection. (D3.1.3-5)

**D4:** Present a summary of arguments and explanations to others outside the classroom using print and oral technologies (e.g., posters, essays, letters, debates, speeches, and reports) and digital technologies (e.g., Internet, social media, and digital documentary). (D4.3.3-5)

*This lesson can also be adapted for use in Grades 6–8 to achieve the comparable C3 objectives for that grade band.*

| **Grade Level**<br>3–5 and higher | **Resources**<br>Primary sources cited in chapter; teacher tools and other resources on the Library of Congress website. | **Time Required**<br>2 days |
| --- | --- | --- |

# Introduction and Connections to the C3 Framework

A newspaper headline just after the death of Susan B. Anthony in 1906 proclaimed "Senate Praises Miss Anthony," but there's a historical irony lurking behind the story.

The same New York State Senate that lauded Anthony for her work to gain "equal political rights for women" denied women the right to vote, and continued to do so for 14 years after her death, until the passage of the 19th Amendment to the U.S. Constitution finally forced the senators to change their position. The article's subheadline mentioned that at least one New York State Senator opposed the resolution, and the section of the newspaper in which the article appeared might indicate whether the editors considered this a story of universal interest. (You can read this article in "Chronicling America" from the Library of Congress at http://chroniclingamerica.loc.gov/lccn/sn83030214/1906-03-14/ed-1/seq-4/)

Primary sources, such as the 1906 newspaper article about Anthony's accomplishments, have a unique power to draw us into historical events. Historical newspapers, photographs, correspondence, and accounts by eyewitnesses can plunge us into the tension and jubilation of historical events and political movements such as the fight for women's suffrage. These sources enable us to see women picketing outside President Wilson's White House, or allow us to visit the grim jail cells of suffragists serving sentences for these peaceful actions. Barring the invention of a time machine, working with primary sources is the closest we will come to being there.

However, the ability these sources have to immerse us in the past is also what requires that we handle them with care. Historical documents can allow us to see an event through a participant's eyes, but we always have to be aware that the perspective is a limited one, shaped by the participant's own background, biases, or access to information. Examining other sources might tell a very different story about the esteem in which Anthony was held by authorities in New York.

For students, primary source analysis is a powerful way to consider perspective. Furthermore, when students analyze historical sources, they engage in a process of careful observation, reflection, and questioning that can build critical thinking skills and promote the construction of new knowledge.

The Library of Congress provides access to millions of historical sources online, as well as teacher tools to support learning. One of these is a primary source analysis tool that is structured to lead students through the independent analysis of sources by helping to organize and structure their thoughts as they record their questions, observations, and reflections, and identify topics for further investigation (see http://www.loc.gov/teachers/primary-source-analysis-tool/).

This chapter explores ways to combine the Library's tools and strategies for primary source analysis with the C3 Framework's Inquiry Arc. The activities described in this lesson will help students examine the changing roles of women in civic life and explore the tactics suffrage activists used to accomplish lasting social change. Students will look at the tactics of the suffrage movement not only as a means of understanding their legacy, but also to make connections to methods of civic engagement that are prevalent and emerging today in the U.S. and beyond.

Woman Suffrage
Picket Parade, 1917,
Library of Congress.

HTTP://WWW.LOC.
GOV/PICTURES/
COLLECTION/HEC/ITEM/
HEC2008007301/

# Inquiry Arc

## Dimension 1: Developing Questions and Planning Inquiries

The first Dimension in the C3 Framework focuses on students' ability to develop their own compelling questions within the constraints of the topical focus of a lesson. In turn, these compelling questions can lead students to consider supporting questions that will drive inquiries forward in a concrete way.

Examining historical photographs is an especially effective way to enter into an inquiry on the women's suffrage movement in the early 20th century, as it can provide just enough information for students to develop questions and plan further inquiries around this increasingly public movement. To begin this lesson, invite students to analyze a photograph of suffragists in a picket line. Guide students' thinking with the Library's primary source analysis tool and encourage them to start asking questions about the photograph.

Initial questions prompted by this photograph might include:

- Who were the activists?
- What tactics did activists in the 20th-century women's suffrage movement use?
- How did those outside the movement react to the protests?
- Who was the audience for the activists' messages? Why might they have chosen that audience?

This introductory activity can lead to a deeper exploration of the tactics used by suffrage activists, and can move students toward posing compelling questions to frame their inquiry. One example of a compelling question students might develop is: *Why did the suffragists choose public protest tactics?*

This question does not have a clear answer, so students must grapple with complex ideas and information. It also meets two important criteria for compelling questions. First, it reflects a social concern about ways to effect change. The question explores choices made by those in the suffrage movement to promote their cause. Second, the question reflects an enduring issue in the field of civics: How do citizens bring about change?

Supporting questions following from this compelling question might include:

- What less public methods did suffragists previously use?
- Were any particular tactics more widely used at specific times during the struggle than others?
- What was the public reaction to the suffragists' public actions?
- How did the government's, or the public's, reaction to the protests affect the suffragists' tactics?
- What methods did opponents of the suffragists use to intimidate or counteract the movement?

After students generate compelling and supporting questions, they can begin gathering historical documents to determine which types of sources will be most helpful in answering their questions.

Historical sources can be found in a wide range of formats, from personal diaries to eyewitness accounts to government reports, and each was created with a specific purpose in mind. It is safe to say, however, that none were created for the purpose of helping today's students answer research questions.

Indicator D1.5.3-5 calls on students to "determine the kinds of sources that will be helpful in answering compelling and supporting questions, taking into consideration the different opinions people have about how to answer the questions." In support of this indicator and because the answers to students' questions will not leap from the page, students may struggle with deciding whether the information available from a particular primary source is helpful. They can evaluate the usefulness of a historical document by asking a series of questions:

- Does the item address an idea or concept related to my compelling or supporting questions?
- Does the item offer a unique point of view that differs from the point of view offered by other items I have consulted?
- Does the item connect to my questions clearly enough to be evident to someone else?
- Does the item add to the "big picture" I am forming about an event or era in order to answer both supporting and compelling questions?

Part of the Vast Billboard Campaign of the Woman's Party. Putting up billboard in Denver—1916, Library of Congress. HTTP://WWW.LOC.GOV/ITEM/MNWP000345/

For this lesson, students can apply the questions to this photograph of a suffrage billboard in Colorado. The goal is to decide if the photograph is helpful in answering either compelling or supporting questions about the tactics used by the women's suffrage movement.

For example, students might answer "yes" to the first question, observing that this photograph shows a persuasive billboard, which is a different tactic than the picket shown in the first photo. For the second question, the answer might be "no," since, like the first photograph the point of view presented is in favor of votes for women. However, another student might say the perspective is different, since the intended audience is different: In the former, the audience is President Wilson, and in the latter the women of Colorado.

For the third question, the answer would likely be "yes." Because the billboard clearly relates to the fight for the right to vote for women, little explanation would be necessary for someone to see its use in seeking answers to the compelling and supporting questions. For the fourth question, the item adds a layer of knowledge to what the researcher already knows about the tactics of the suffragists, since it shows the use of slogans, billboards, and anti-Wilson arguments. Because all four questions could be answered in the affirmative, the verdict would be in favor of the photograph as a helpful source.

Students can further develop these skills by asking questions about the historical documents found in the Women's Suffrage Primary Source Set from the Library of Congress at http://www.loc.gov/teachers/classroommaterials/primarysourcesets/womens-suffrage/.

Dimension 2 of the C3 framework asks students to develop historians' habits, including sourcing and contextualizing items, in pursuit of the answers to compelling and supporting questions. Ultimately, the C3 framework expects that students determine the usefulness of a source in an inquiry. Indicator 13 in the history subsection of Dimension 2 asks students to "use information about a historical source, including the maker, date, place of origin, intended audience, and purpose to judge the extent to which the source is useful for studying a particular topic." (D2.His.13.3-5) In this part of the lesson, students will practice this skill by analyzing another photograph—one related to the opposition to women's suffrage.

In order to "use information about an historical source" as the C3 framework suggests, to think about the document's creator, and to situate the document in time and place, students can ask a series of questions.

- Who created the document? What role did the creator have in the event?
- When was the item created in relation to the time of the events?
- Who was the item's intended audience?
- What was the item's intended purpose?
- What was happening when the item was created?
- Who played important roles in the event?

National Anti-Suffrage Association c.1911, Library of Congress.


Looking at primary sources as a historian would and asking questions such as these prevents students from accepting sources as representative of the entire truth about an event or era. Firsthand evidence can be invaluable in the study of history, as it has not been filtered through the perspective of someone who was not a participant. However, all historical sources come with their own context and history, and working with historical sources requires that students act carefully and responsibly. Invite students to look closely at the photograph "National Anti-Suffrage Association," and ask how it can add to their understanding of the struggle for women's suffrage. Encourage students to answer the sourcing questions above as they examine the photograph, and direct them to consult the bibliographic record or other information available about the item. (A bibliographic record accompanies most items available digitally from the Library of Congress. Look for "About this item" to find the bibliographic information.)

Ask students how valuable this photograph is in building their understanding of the suffrage movement. Remind them that analyzing additional primary sources adds layers to their knowledge while they continue their inquiry.

Historical sources can represent dramatically different points of view, and sometimes provide contradictory accounts of events. Evaluating multiple sources and determining their value as evidence is an important part of the C3 framework's inquiry arc.

Historical sources documenting suffragists' actions provide opportunities for students to weigh evidence from multiple perspectives. Indicator D3.1.3-5 emphasizes this point by suggesting that students "gather relevant information from multiple sources while using the origin, structure, and context to guide the selection."

For example, while developing an answer to the supporting question "What tactics did activists in the suffrage movement use?" students might use additional photographs from the Library's online collections. Visual evidence of suffragists' methods can be found by searching the Library's collections using keywords such as "suffrage," "women's suffrage," or other related terms. Many sources are available in the Miller NAWSA Suffrage Scrapbooks, which are available on the Library website at http://www.loc.gov/search/?q=Miller+NAWSA+Suffrage+Scrapbooks%2C+1897-1911&fa=partof%3Amiller+nawsa+suffrage+scrapbooks%2C+1897-1911. (You can also access them by entering "Miller NAWSA" into the website's search engine.)

These photographic sources alone do not offer a complete picture of the methods used by suffragists or their opponents. Acquiring another layer of corroborative evidence from additional historical sources can only strengthen students' thinking.

Newspaper articles and personal correspondence invite students to look closely for specific methods used by the suffrage movement. While these documents might seem to provide straightforward evidence, students still should consider the circumstances of these documents' creation, and what biases need to be considered when using them in an inquiry. By continuing to add to the layers of evidence, students build a solid foundation to construct an argument to answer the supporting question. Information from these historical sources may send students back to items they have seen previously or to new items for corroborating and additional depth. For example, primary sources on the preparations for demonstrations, or on the hunger strikes and force-feeding of suffragists will offer students compelling insights into the intensity of the struggle for women's suffrage. (See, for example, the letter from Nora Blatch De Forest to Anne Fitzhugh Miller asking for support for an upcoming demonstration at http://www.loc.gov/item/rbcmiller002554, or the newspaper report on this page, "Alice Paul Describes Force Feeding," at http://www.loc.gov/item/rbcmiller003904.)

---

## ...eing Fed Through Nostrils Is Described by Alice Paul, Young American Suffragette

### Inventor of Hunger Strike Tells How British Prison Physicians Keep Life in Women Who Won't Eat or Wear Clothes.

London, Dec. 9.—Miss Alice Paul, of Philadelphia, the suffragette who was arrested November 9th and sentenced to a month's hard labor for her share in the suffragette demonstration at the Lord Mayor's banquet at the Guildhall, was released from Holloway jail this morning on the completion of her thirty days. She left the prison in a cab, accompanied by two wardresses, and went to the home of friends. A doctor was immediately called to attend her there, owing to her weakened condition.

Miss Paul, who was the inventor of the suffragettes' "hunger strike" and practiced it during her latest term in jail, was cheerful, and said she did not regret her conduct, and was prepared to repeat it again if necessary. She said she was unable to undergo the ordeal of an interview, but later she sent your correspondent a statement by a friend. On previous convictions, Miss Paul was able to gain her freedom by refusing to eat, but her tactics were futile this time.

Miss Paul said she was the granddaughter of a New Jersey judge, and a master of arts of the University of Pennsylvania. She had done a great deal of settlement work during the last four years, and came to London in September, 1908, to study economics. After saying that she was first struck by the contrast between the academic interest in woman suffrage in America and the lively character of the movement here, Miss Paul told this story of her prison life.

"I practiced a hunger strike until November 11th. After that date they fed me twice a day by force, except on one day when I was too ill to be touched. I have no complaints against the Holloway officials. I spent the whole time in bed, because I refused to wear prison clothes.

"Each day, I was wrapped in blankets and taken to another cell to be fed, the food being injected through my nostrils.

"During this operation the largest wardress in Holloway sat astride my knees, holding my shoulders down to keep me from bending forward. Two other wardresses sat on either side and held my arms. Then a towel was placed around my throat, and one doctor from behind forced my head back, while another doctor put a tube in my nostril. When it reached my throat my head was pushed forward.

"Twice the tube came through my mouth and I got it between my teeth. My mouth was then pried open with an instrument. Sometimes they tied me to a chair with sheets. Once I managed to get my hands loose and snatched the tube, tearing it with my teeth. I also broke a jug, but I didn't give in."

Miss Paul lives alone in London. Her friend told me with great gusto how Miss Paul had eluded the vigilance of the police at the Lord Mayor's banquet. It seems she and Miss Amelia Brown, her partner in the escapade, dressed as charwomen, went to the Guildhall at 9 o'clock in the morning. Every time they met anyone they asked the way to the kitchen. They had many hairbreadth escapes, and once, seeing a policeman close at hand, they knelt down to escape notice. In the dark the policeman actually put his cape on them. Finally they succeeded in getting to the gallery overlooking the banqueting hall, where they shrieked and threw stones through a stained glass window.

Miss Lucy Burns, the other American suffragette, is following Winston Spencer Churchill around the country, making it as warm as possible for the President of the Board of Trade.

---

When considering where to search for historical information to fill gaps and deepen understanding, a number of questions can guide students:

- What do I still need to know about the event or time to supplement what I already know?
- What additional perspectives are needed to ensure I have considered both (or many) sides of the story?
- Do I need to corroborate the factual information provided by this item?
- Should I look for other types of items, such as newspapers, photographs, journals, letters, and others?

## Dimension 4: Communicating Conclusions and Taking Informed Action

The study of a transformational social movement like the campaign for women's suffrage can have an impact beyond the classroom door.

The suffrage pioneers didn't safeguard their ideas within the walls of their homes and meeting halls. Instead, they took to the streets, using innovative tactics and emerging media to spread their message in the public sphere.

As students come to the close of their inquiry into the tactics of the suffragists, it's only appropriate that they consider using similarly innovative methods to communicate their own conclusions. Given that indicator D4.3.3-5 calls on students to create summaries of "arguments and explanations to others outside the classroom" using various print, oral, and digital techniques, students might look at the mass media of the suffrage era, such as penny newspapers and motion pictures, and use today's newest communications tools to present the results of their investigation.

At the same time, however, close inquiry into the history of social change can help students see the power and the possibilities for their own civic activism. Women's right to vote was won through protest, petition, and patriotism. After a study of the fight for suffrage, ask students what causes they would be willing to fight for today, and what means they might use to bring about change.

You might lead students from an analysis of the suffragists' methods to a critique of the tactics used by activists today. Help them brainstorm the most effective ways to change people's minds, and avenues for seeking redress of their own grievances. Make sure they are familiar with the laws and policies governing political action and protests. And remind them that the United States is the nation that it is today only through the efforts of engaged, informed citizens.

There may be no better way to help students see the possibilities and the rewards of becoming participatory citizens than through the study of the historical traces left by the activists of the past. Working with historical sources can help students analyze and understand the people and events that make up the nation's history, but it can also help them see the power to make history that lies within them.

# About the Library of Congress

The mission of the Library of Congress is to support the Congress in fulfilling its constitutional duties and to further the progress of knowledge and creativity for the benefit of the American people.

The Library of Congress is the repository of millions of primary source items relevant to the study of American history and civics. Many of these items have been digitized and are therefore freely available to teachers and students across the United States and the world. Working with primary sources not only engages students in subject matter, but can also help them build their critical thinking skills and construct new knowledge.

The Library's educational outreach mission is to promote the effective classroom use of the Library's primary sources. To do so, it provides teaching tools and professional development on its online home for teachers, http://loc.gov/teachers. It also provides face-to-face professional development through workshops and teacher institutes, and is building a nationwide consortium of partner institutions.

For additional resources, please visit the following:
- The Library of Congress:
  http://loc.gov
- The Library of Congress Teachers page:
  http://loc.gov/teachers
- Primary Source Analysis Tool:
  http://www.loc.gov/teachers/primary-source-analysis-tool/
- Primary Source Set: Women's Suffrage
  http://www.loc.gov/teachers/classroommaterials/primarysourcesets/womens-suffrage/
- Twitter:
  @TeachingLC

*The authors of this chapter are Cheryl Lederle, Educational Resource Specialist at the Library of Congress; Rebecca Newland, Library of Congress 2013-2015 Teacher in Residence; and Stephen Wesson, Educational Resource Specialist at the Library of Congress.*

# Do Our Choices **Matter?**
## The Fragility of Democracy

**Facing History and Ourselves**

**Facing History and Ourselves**

| **C3 Disciplinary Focus**<br>World History, Civics | **C3 Inquiry Focus**<br>Developing questions and using sources to construct explanations | **Content Topic**<br>The Holocaust and human behavior |
|---|---|---|

**C3 Focus Indicators**

**D1:** Explain how supporting questions contribute to an inquiry and how, through engaging source work, new compelling and supporting questions emerge. (D1.4.9-12)

**D2:** Evaluate public policies in terms of intended and unintended outcomes, and related consequences. (D2.Civ.13.9-12)

**D2:** Analyze multiple and complex causes and effects of events in the past. (D2.His.14.9-12)

**D3:** Gather relevant information from multiple sources representing a wide range of views. (D3.1.9-12)

**D4:** Construct arguments using precise and knowledgeable claims, with evidence from multiple sources, while acknowledging counterclaims and evidentiary weaknesses. (D4.1.9-12)

**D4:** Assess options for individual and collective action to address local, regional and global problems by engaging in self-reflection, strategy identification and complex causal reasoning. (D4.7.9-12)

| **Grade Level**<br>9–12 | **Resources**<br>Resources cited in the chapter; Facing History and Ourselves website. | **Time Required**<br>3 days—within a larger unit of study |
|---|---|---|

# Introduction and Connections to the C3 Framework



**—Sonia Weitz, from her poem, "For Yom Ha'Shoah"**

In seeking to understand the "why" Sonia Weitz identifies, Facing History and Ourselves invites teachers to guide students through a journey along the C3 Inquiry Arc.

This journey consists of a series of lessons about choices in the past and present. By exploring questions about the choices which individuals, groups, and nations confronted through the history of Germany in the 1920s and 1930s, students reflect upon a few key themes:

- Our choices matter.
- History is not inevitable. Democracies are dynamic institutions that change according to the decisions of the individuals and groups of institutions within them.

We use readings from our primary resource book, *Facing History and Ourselves: Holocaust and Human Behavior*, to create a complex, multi-layered study of history. These documents facilitate students' development of historical thinking skills and civic engagement — questioning, analysis, evaluating evidence, and taking informed action — by providing them with rich and diverse primary and secondary historical texts. Students are encouraged to go beyond monolithic explanations of historical events, and ask deep, probing questions to understand how a particular set of circumstances came about. Readings from multiple perspectives, which students are asked to evaluate and analyze, help them to see that individuals' beliefs and actions are often influenced, although not determined, by what is happening around them. They identify multiple causes for events and understand the power needed to resist or change events in their own lives. Linking past and present, they learn to put themselves in others' shoes, which helps them think deeply about the choices and decisions made by individuals, groups, and nations. Reading accounts of ordinary citizens can offer perspectives to reflect upon their own practice of civic life.

A typical Facing History unit, which engages students in the critical examination of history, spans approximately four to six weeks and is guided by a compelling question. Within this larger inquiry arc, there may be many smaller segments of inquiry. Each layer of inquiry pushes students to go deeper into the history and deeper into their own thinking.

# Inquiry Arc

Facing History units are often called journeys, and they begin with a compelling question. For this unit, the teacher introduces the compelling question, *Do our choices matter?* This frames the initial trajectory of the overall inquiry arc. By setting this framing, the teacher also provides space for students to journal and brainstorm their own questions around choices and consequences. The additional questions that arise through this process will enhance and help guide the class through the Facing History journey.

The scope and sequence of a Facing History unit (see Figure 1) presents many opportunities for students to develop questions as they grapple with a set of episodes in history and their meaning for today.

This chapter presents one inquiry within the larger arc. The full unit will have many such layers of inquiry. Each smaller inquiry stands on its own and develops a culture of questioning which is critical to student development of civic engagement.

The smaller inquiry presented here takes the overall question of "Do our choices matter?" and guides students to focus on the choices made by German citizens during the 1920s and 1930s in Germany. Students ask what choices ordinary Germans made regarding a religious minority increasingly marginalized in their society and why (Dimension 1). They then build a historical context for this question by synthesizing and activating prior learning from the unit and expanding their understanding of the context in which choices were made (Dimension 2). With this background, students then explore primary sources from the time period to discern multiple perspectives — a range of answers to the question of what choices ordinary Germans made and why (Dimension 3). Finally, students consider the consequences of the choices made at that time, and the implications for choices we may confront in our own day. This builds students' sense of civic agency as they recognize the impact that decisions they make can have within their own peer groups and their wider communities (Dimension 4).

**FIGURE 1**

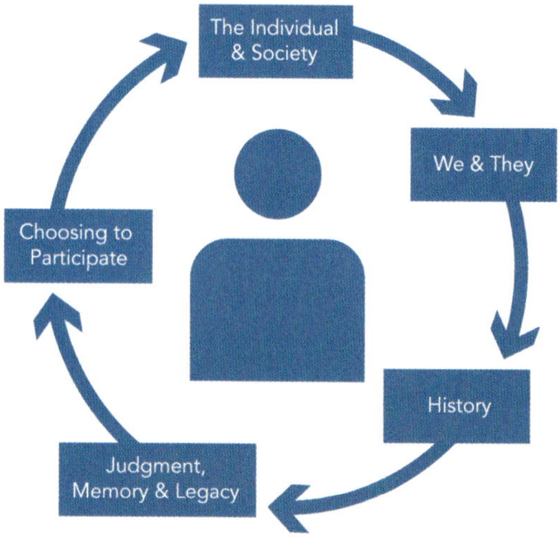


## Dimension 1: Developing Questions and Planning Inquiries

For the purposes of this chapter, we will examine a "mini-inquiry" within a unit on the collapse of democracy in post-World War I Germany in the years leading to the Holocaust. To give context, this inquiry will come after students have studied the significance of the Treaty of Versailles and the societal conditions in Weimar Germany, which allowed the Nazi Party to gain followers and eventually achieve a majority of the seats in the Reichstag. Students will also, in a Facing History class, have already considered the complexity of identity and the way our identity—and the way in which the identity of others is defined—influences our choices. The compelling question for this mini-inquiry is, "What choices were available to ordinary German citizens in the 1920s and 1930s, and how did the range of choices narrow as the Nazis gained power?"

In a Facing History classroom, students are encouraged to journal regularly as this is one strategy for encouraging students to ponder compelling questions, develop supporting questions, and strengthen the habit of questioning that will push them to engage more deeply with the material. In this way, students are invited to exercise their capacities for moral reasoning and help direct the course of questioning in a classroom. For suggested prompts and uses of a journal, see http://www.facinghistory.org/journals-facing-history-class.

By considering the events of the 1920s in Germany and the election of the Nazi party, students naturally turn to the question of the choices made by individuals in Germany and the pressures imposed by the Nazi Party as it consolidated power. Student journaling and discussion turns to questions such as:

- Did everybody turn against the Jews?
- How did individuals justify the violence they saw around them?
- Why did people accept the Nazi dismantling of democracy that took place in the 1930s?
- What conditions need to be present in a society for neighbor to turn against neighbor?

These student-generated questions and the mini-inquiry focus contribute to making the compelling question of "Do our choices matter?" even more complex and nuanced. In this way, students can see and begin to "explain how supporting questions contribute to an inquiry and how, through engaging source work, new compelling and supporting questions emerge." (D1.4.9-12) Questions that arise can help students not only think deeply about the choices that exist in the history, but also make connections between the case study and their own roles as civic agents in society today.

## Dimension 2: Connections to Disciplinary Tools and Concepts

It is important within Dimension 2 to ground students in the historical time period. In the two exercises below, students (1) analyze a painting to synthesize the material previously studied and build contextual knowledge for the place and time period in which German citizens were confronting and making the choices that were open to them as the Nazi Party was becoming established in Germany, and (2) create a human timeline to recognize the small steps that took place over time to dismantle German democracy. Through both of these exercises, they build the essential background knowledge that will become the foundation for students to "analyze multiple and complex causes and effects of events in the past." (D2.His.14.9-12)

*Der Agitator* by George Grosz

© ESTATE OF GEORGE GROSZ/LICENSED BY VAGA, NEW YORK, NY

This painting from George Grosz (1928) can be used to help students synthesize what they have learned about the instability and threats to democracy that characterized the Weimar Republic. Through close viewing of the painting and connection to the history they have previously studied, students will articulate key elements of the German society at the time the Nazi Party came to power.

Students can be guided through a close media analysis of this image.

1.  What are the concrete objects you see in this painting? (Shapes, colors, objects—refraining at the beginning from making any assumptions or interpretations.)

2.  What questions does this painting raise for you? (This is an important step to reinforce the importance of questioning in our learning.)

3.  What additional information can we bring to bear to understand this painting? (This is an opportunity to specifically bring in details from previous mini-inquiries within the unit. There is an entire online module on the Weimar Republic, which is helpful for students to explore and would be the basis for additional information students are synthesizing in the analysis of this painting. It can be accessed at https://www.facinghistory.org/weimar)

4.  Given this additional information, what might the artist's message be? (And what in the painting supports that interpretation?)

Once the Nazi Party entered the Reichstag in 1932, Hitler and the Nazi leadership acted quickly to dismantle democracy, rebuild Germany, and destroy enemies. They did this through cultural and social steps as much as political and military. It is important for students to see these small steps. One way to do this is through a Human Timeline of the 1930s in Germany. An example of this strategy is available at https://www.facinghistory.org/human-timeline.

In this strategy, students are given specific events or laws passed from 1932 to 1939 that show actions taken by Nazi leadership. These should specifically include laws that restricted Jewish participation in German society—well-known legislation such as the Nuremberg laws and lesser-known acts such as restricting who could be a government employee or who could own radios. This will help students identify the pressures that defined the society of Nazi Germany in which individuals made their choices.

Building historical context with these activities helps students "analyze multiple and complex causes and effects of events in the past" (D2.His.14.9-12) and "evaluate public policies in terms of intended and unintended outcomes, and related consequences." (D.2.Civ.13.9-12)

# Dimension 3: Evaluating Sources and Using Evidence

As students read sources from 1933–1945, they will investigate the diversity of choices available to some individuals and the lack of choices available to others. It is important to note that during this time period the range of choices and roles that individuals and groups had available to them was different than during the Weimar years. As they come to recognize and appreciate that difference, students engage in additional critical thinking discussions and activities to more fully understand the context of choice-making during the Holocaust.

Below are three individuals who made choices about how to respond to the violence of Kristallnacht. With the historical background already discussed, students are ready to engage critically in the inquiry about the choices available to ordinary German citizens in the 1920s and 1930s, and how the range of choices narrowed as the Nazis gained power.

**ALFONS HECK, FORMER MEMBER OF THE HITLER YOUTH**

> Far from being forced to enter the ranks of the Jungvolk, I could barely contain my impatience and was, in fact, accepted before I was quite 10. It seemed like an exciting life, free from parental supervision, filled with "duties" that seemed sheer pleasure. Precision marching was something one could endure for hiking, camping, war games in the field, and a constant emphasis on sports... To a degree, our prewar activities resembled those of the Boy Scouts, with much more emphasis on discipline and political indoctrination. There were the paraphernalia and the symbols, the pomp and the mysticism, very close in feeling to religious rituals. One of the first significant demands was the so-called Mutprobe: "test of courage," which was usually administered after a six-month period of probation. The members of my Schar, a platoon-like unit of about 40-50 boys, were required to dive off the three-meter board—about 10 feet high—head first in the town's swimming pool. There were some stinging belly flops, but the pain was worth it when our Fahnleinfuehrer, the 15-year-old leader of our Fahnlein (literally "little flag"), a company-like unit of about 160 boys, handed us the coveted dagger with its inscription Blood and Honor. From that moment on we were fully accepted.

To hear Alfons Heck describe his response to Kristallnacht and to the deportation of Jews from his hometown, watch *Heil Hitler: Confessions of a Hitler Youth*. Facing History educators can borrow this from our library at https://www.facinghistory.org/resources/heil-hitler-confessions-hitler-youth.

**MELITA MASCHMANN**

Melita lived in a small suburb of Berlin and knew nothing of Kristallnacht until the next morning. As she picked her way through the broken glass on her way to work, she asked a policeman what had happened. After he explained, she recalls:

> I went on my way shaking my head. For the space of a second I was clearly aware that something terrible had happened there. Something frighteningly

Maschmann was not alone in placing the night in perspective. Dietrich Goldschmidt, a minister in the Confessing Church, explains that for most Germans "the persecution of the Jews, this escalating persecution of the Jews, and the 9th of November—in a sense, that was only one event, next to very many gratifying ones. Here the famous stories of all the things Hitler did come in: 'He got rid of unemployment, he built the Autobahn, the people started doing well again, he restored our national pride again. One has to weigh that against the other things.'"

**ANDRE**

It was the autumn of 1938. Andre was twelve years old and lived with his parents in a small town in northern Germany. One evening he came home from his youth movement meeting.



Their conversation proceeded, the son presenting questions to his father, the father turning the questions back to his son.



When Andre returned a short while later, he approached his parents, who were sitting at the table.

And that is what they did. The following day, Andre's family left Germany.

• • •

All of these, and many other readings, can be found in the *Facing History and Ourselves: Holocaust and Human Behavior* resource book, available for free download at https://www. facinghistory.org/resources/facing-history-and-ourselves-holocaust-and-human-behavior.

After exploring theses sources, teachers should return to a sample of student-created supporting questions:

- Did everybody turn against the Jews?
- How did individuals justify the violence they saw around them?
- Why did people accept the Nazi dismantling of democracy that took place in the 1930s?
- What conditions need to be present in a society for neighbor to turn against neighbor?

These primary sources give multiple perspectives for students to consider in their own questions as well as our mini-inquiry question, "What choices were available to ordinary German citizens in the 1920s and 1930s, and how did the range of choices narrow as the Nazis gained power?" They also contribute to a rich and nuanced response to our larger unit question of "Do our choices matter?" Through this process of deep investigation and analysis, we encourage students to listen carefully to the stories each source tells, to continue to add more contextual information to deepen their understanding of the history, and to reflect deeply about what these sources mean for the compelling questions about humanity and agency. By doing so, students practice C3 skills, such as "Gather relevant information from multiple sources representing a wide range of views." (D3.1.9-12)

## Dimension 4: Communicating Conclusions and Taking Informed Action

To conclude this mini-inquiry, students could write their own response to the question, *What choices were available to ordinary German citizens in the 1920s and 1930s, and how did the range of choices narrow as the Nazis gained power?* This engages them in articulating what they saw in the evidence, how they reconcile the choices made within that context, and how they recognize the moral implications of those choices and the significant consequences of those choices.

As students identify how choices mattered during the years leading to the Holocaust and what range of choices were available to individuals, groups, and nations during this history, they balance these understandings with speculations about human behavior, and so reflect upon the different levels of intricacy that may go into a person's individual choice. (The psychology of human behavior might in and of itself be a mini-inquiry along the larger Inquiry Arc if time allows.) Students can now recognize that violence and injustice often begin with small steps of indifference, conformity, acceptance, and not thinking about what is happening. Additional readings such as "No Time to Think" might be shared to compare students' own writing about this question with the thoughts of somebody who lived through the experience and reflects back on the actions and inactions of German citizens. (See https://www.facinghistory.org/no-time-think.)

In their journals and class discussions, students discuss what words like perpetrator, victim, and bystander mean in the context of both everyday and extreme situations. At the same time, they begin to understand that these terms are dynamic, and that at different times throughout an event, people make all types of choices and may play the role of bystander one day and perpetrator or victim the next. This will help them write their own analysis for the mini-inquiry question. In doing this, students "construct arguments using precise and knowledgeable claims, with evidence from multiple sources, while acknowledging counterclaims and evidentiary weaknesses." (D4.1.9-12)

This analysis will also lead directly into future mini-inquiries as students grapple directly with the consequences by looking at the steps taken next in the years leading to the Holocaust. As they realize that this history is about far more than a person or group simply being "evil," and encompassed a whole series of choices and actions that eventually led to catastrophe and genocide, students may well come to understand that history is not inevitable and that crimes against humanity are rooted in a confluence of specific attitudes, choices, and circumstances.

As a result of this inquiry, students reflect upon connections to their own choices in their schools, communities, and democracies, a process that can encourage civic participation and a recognition by students that their choices matter.

While we introduce students to acts of informed participation and civic engagement throughout the case study, as the full Inquiry wraps up, it is valuable to spend some focused time here for students to "assess options for individual and collective action to address local, regional, and global problems by engaging in self-reflection, strategy identification, and complex causal reasoning." (D4.7.9-12) To accomplish this, teachers can give students space to reflect on the concept of Choosing to Participate in the context of their own identities and communities.

During Choosing to Participate, students are encouraged to ask questions like, "What issues are confronting me and my community? What actions might I take to participate?" The goal of these final lessons is not to force or even propel students into action. Instead, it is to open up their eyes to the different types of participation happening around them and provide a space for them to reflect on who they are, who they want to be, and what kind of world they want to create.

Students might spend time learning about examples of student participation, such as videos produced during the "Not In Our Schools" project (http://www.niot.org/nios), that illustrate student responses to injustice. They might meet current leaders at universities or in their communities to understand what propels people to decide to make a difference. At times, a Facing History class may decide to engage in a project to target an issue in their school. If this happens, a teacher may engage students in an exercise to examine strategies used in historical or contemporary examples of participation.

However, it would be equally valid for a student to simply begin to think differently about how he or she interacts with a classmate or family member. Facing History values a wide range of participation and believes that the small, often invisible steps toward creating a just society are as important as the ones that receive accolades and chapters in future history texts.

Ultimately, we hope to create a society of thoughtful citizens who think deeply about the way they live, as much when they are riding the subway to work as when they hear about a national disaster that needs aid. Indeed, at the end of the unit, we hope students believe their choices do matter and are compelled to think carefully about the decisions they make, realizing that their choices will ultimately shape the world.

# About Facing History and Ourselves

Facing History and Ourselves is an organization created in 1976 by educators who believed that instilling intellectual vigor and curiosity as well as developing emotional learning and ethical judgment must all be part of the teaching of historical content.

We provide training, professional development, and resources that support the practical needs and the spirits of educators worldwide who share the goal of creating a better, more informed, and more thoughtful society. Visit http://facinghistory.org to learn more and download all the resources mentioned in this chapter.

*The authors of this chapter are Mary Hendra, Associate Program Director for Los Angeles and Organizational Innovation, and Jocelyn Stanton, Senior Associate for Program Staff Development at Facing History and Ourselves. The copyright of this chapter is owned by Facing History and Ourselves. © 2014 Facing History and Ourselves.*

# CHAPTER 10

# Why Do We Call It The "Great" Depression?

**The Federal Reserve Bank of St. Louis**

Migrant family looking for work in the pea fields of California.
PHOTOGRAPH BY DOROTHEA LANGE, 1935. FROM FDR PRESIDENTIAL LIBRARY.

| Federal Reserve Bank of St. Louis, Research Division—Economic Education | | |
| --- | --- | --- |
| **C3 Disciplinary Focus** Economics | **C3 Inquiry Focus** Using disciplinary concepts to evaluate evidence and construct explanations | **Content Topic** The Great Depression |

**C3 Focus Indicators**

**D1:** Explain points of agreement and disagreement experts have about interpretations and applications of disciplinary concepts and ideas associated with a supporting question. (D1.3.9-12)

**D2:** Use benefits and costs to evaluate the effectiveness of government policies to improve market outcomes. (D2.Eco.7.9-12)

**D3:** Gather relevant information from multiple sources representing a wide range of views while using the origin, authority, structure, context, and corroborative value of the sources to guide the selection. (D3.1.9-12)

**D4:** Construct explanations using sound reasoning, correct sequence (linear or non-linear), examples, and details with significant and pertinent information and data, while acknowledging the strengths and weaknesses of the explanation given its purpose (e.g., cause and effect, chronological, procedural, technical). (D4.2.9-12)

| **Grade Level** 9–12 | **Resources** Resources cited in this chapter and the Federal Reserve Bank of St. Louis' Great Depression website | **Time Required** 2–3 days |
| --- | --- | --- |

# Introduction and Connections to the C3 Framework

Ask your students what they know about the Great Depression, and they will likely respond that it was caused by the Stock Market Crash of 1929, and that it ended as a result of an alphabet soup of New Deal programs. The content in their history textbooks likely reflects this level of misinformation. When introduced to the study of the Great Depression students are likely to ask: why should we study or care about the Great Depression—an event that affected our great-grandparents? Shouldn't we focus on more recent events?

How can you help your students understand why they should study this watershed event? How can your students move beyond the simplistic and inaccurate assessment of its causes and solutions to gain a deeper understanding of the factors that caused the Great Depression and its impact on the American people and on the U.S. economy? How can you help them learn to use economic tools to analyze the impact of other events and policies on the U.S. economy, including the most recent economic crisis, the Great Recession?

This chapter suggests ideas for guiding students through an inquiry that allows them to think economically and apply concepts from economics, civics, and history to analyze the Great Depression while using the educational resources of the Federal Reserve Bank of St. Louis, which are available on its Great Depression website, to support their understanding. (The overview on pages 104-105 of this chapter is one of many such resources.) This lesson focuses on the compelling question: Why Do We Call It the "Great" Depression? The lesson calls on students to develop supporting questions, investigate those questions using carefully selected sources, and compose explanations in response to the supporting questions.

Eleanor Roosevelt talking with a project superintendent in Des Moines, Iowa. June 8, 1936. This project, sponsored by the Works Progress Administration, planned to convert a city dump into a water front park.

The combination of content resources developed by the Federal Reserve Bank of St. Louis and the C3 Framework provide an opportunity for students to go in search of new knowledge to help them understand and explain the causes of the Great Depression and its impact on the American people. These lessons employ the four dimensions of the C3 inquiry arc over 2-3 class periods with an emphasis on Dimension 2—Connections to Disciplinary Tools and Concepts. The goal of these lessons is to engage students in critical historical thought while utilizing key economic content, data, and primary source material.

# Inquiry Arc

## Dimension 1: Developing Questions and Planning Inquiries

This lesson begins by posing for students the compelling question: *Why Do We Call It the "Great" Depression?* Although students should have regular opportunities to construct their own compelling question, this question represents a common curriculum topic and is sufficiently complex to necessitate a wide range of interesting supporting questions. The lesson develops as students construct supporting questions as they "explain points of agreement and disagreement experts have about interpretations and applications of disciplinary concepts and ideas associated with a supporting question." (D1.3.9-12)

An approach to developing supporting questions for inquiry is first to show your students photographs from the Great Depression found at http://www.stlouisfed. org/great-depression/gallery.html. Ask the students what these photos communicate about this time in our history and what the students already know about the Great Depression. In response to the question about the photos, students might say that people looked poor, tired, desperate, and hungry, and that many were out of work. These initial ideas are a starting place for students to explore some of the more complex concepts and ideas related to the Great Depression. For example, have students compose questions based on the five Ws (who, what, when, where, why):

- Who was affected?
- What caused this hardship?
- Where did this happen?
- Why were there so many people out of work?
- Why wasn't there enough food?
- When did this occur?

From these questions, students might then be asked to consider what they already know about the Great Depression. These ideas might include:

- It was caused by the stock market crash.
- It happened a long time ago and lasted for a long time.
- The New Deal ended the Great Depression.
- World War II ended the Great Depression.
- Farmers destroyed crops, milk, and other products.
- Banks were closed.

The compelling question that is our focus, "Why Do We Call It the 'Great' Depression?" can lead to supporting questions, such as:

- What is a depression?
- How did we know this was a depression?
- How did it compare to previous depressions?

From these questions, students can move into data related to measuring the economy—such as real GDP, unemployment, and inflation. They can use these data to compare the period of the Great Depression with other crises and with more normal periods since 1929. Once students have their supporting questions, they can examine points of agreement and disagreement that experts have concerning the related ideas and concepts. In terms of what caused the depression, students may continue by looking at factors that economic historians have investigated as causes for the Great Depression, such as changes in specific industries (agriculture, automobile, housing, banking and finance).

Use the initial questions and the students' knowledge of the Great Depression to guide them to develop other supporting questions.

- How did the Great Depression affect people?
- How did people deal with the Great Depression?
- How is a depression different from a recession?
- What are the indicators used to determine a depression?
- How did the Great Depression end?

Answering these questions will support research by the students investigating a number of compelling questions relating to the Great Depression in addition to the compelling question that is the focus of this chapter. They include:

- What caused the Great Depression?
- What events or policies ended the Great Depression?
- What government or Federal Reserve policies were effective/ineffective?
- How did the Great Depression change the U.S.?

## Dimension 2: Connections to Disciplinary Tools and Concepts

With compelling and supporting questions in place, students could begin to examine points of agreement and disagreement among experts about the Great Depression and the reasons why it had such damaging effects for such a long time. They might consider the impact that policies designed during the Great Depression had on the size of the government and its role in the economy. This should involve evaluating "the selection of monetary and fiscal policies in a variety of economic conditions." (D2.Econ.12.9-12) They could consider incentives established by these policies, including changes related to the banking industry, such as the implementation of the Federal Deposit Insurance Corporation (FDIC); agricultural support policies; and Social Security.

Economists measure the economy by analyzing economic indicators. Ask students if they know what unemployment, inflation, and real gross domestic product are. Point out that understanding what these indicators are and how they are measured provide the basis for understanding the health of the economy now and during the Great Depression. Students can examine "help-wanted" advertising in newspapers in the United States before, during and after the Great Depression. (These and the other indicators mentioned in this paragraph are accessible on the website of the Federal Reserve Bank of St. Louis at http://research.stlouisfed.org/dashboard/440.) Ask what they might conclude regarding help-wanted ads during times of recession (many fewer help-wanted ads). Have students look at graphs of the unemployment rate and ask how the help-wanted ads graph correlates with the unemployment rate graph (lower number of help-wanted ads, higher rates of unemployment). Explain that during recessions, businesses hire fewer workers—and even let workers go. The demand for workers decreases. Show students other graphs, such as the rate of change in real gross domestic product (real GDP) growth, and the percent change in CONTINUED ON PAGE 106

# The Great Depression: An Overview
## by David C. Wheelock

One reason to study the Great Depression is that it was by far the worst economic catastrophe of the 20th century and, perhaps, the worst in our nation's history. Between 1929 and 1933, the quantity of goods and services produced in the United States fell by one-third, the unemployment rate soared to 25 percent of the labor force, the stock market lost 80 percent of its value and some 7,000 banks failed.

At the store, the price of chicken fell from 38 cents a pound to 12 cents, the price of eggs dropped from 50 cents a dozen to just over 13 cents, and the price of gasoline fell from 10 cents a gallon to less than a nickel. Still, many families went hungry, and few could afford to own a car.

Another reason to study the Great Depression is that the sheer magnitude of the economic collapse— and the fact that it involved every aspect of our economy and every region of our country—makes this event a great vehicle for teaching important economic concepts. You can learn about inflation and deflation, Gross Domestic Product (GDP), and unemployment by comparing the Depression with more recent experiences, including the financial crisis and Great Recession of 2007-09. Further, the Great Depression shows the important roles that money, banks and the stock market play in our economy.

A third reason to study the Great Depression is that it dramatically changed the role of government, especially the federal government, in our nation's economy. Before the Great Depression, federal government spending accounted for 3 percent of GDP. By 1939, federal outlays reached 10 percent of GDP.[1] (At present, federal spending accounts for about 20 percent of GDP.) The Great Depression also brought us the Federal Deposit Insurance Corp. (FDIC), regulation of securities markets, the birth of the Social Security System and the first national minimum wage.

## WHAT CAUSED THE GREAT DEPRESSION?

Economists continue to study the Great Depression because they still disagree on what caused it. Many theories have been advanced over the years, and there remains no single, universally agreed-upon explanation as to why the Depression happened or why the economy eventually recovered.

The 1929 stock market crash often comes to mind first when people think about the Great Depression.

The crash destroyed considerable wealth. Perhaps even more important, the crash sparked doubts about the health of the economy, which led consumers and firms to pull back on their spending, especially on big-ticket items like cars and appliances. However, as big as it was, the stock market crash alone did not cause the Great Depression.

Some economists point a finger at protectionist trade policies and the collapse of international trade.

The Smoot-Hawley tariff of 1930 dramatically increased the cost of imported goods and led to retaliatory actions by the United States' major trading partners. The Great Depression was a worldwide phenomenon, and the collapse of international trade was even greater than the collapse of world output of goods and services. Still, like the stock market crash, protectionist trade policies alone did not cause the Great Depression.

Other experts offer different explanations for the Great Depression. Some historians have called the Depression an inevitable failure of capitalism. Others blame the Depression on the "excesses" of the 1920s: excessive production of commodities, excessive building, excessive financial speculation or an excessively skewed distribution of income and wealth. None of these explanations has held up very well over time. One explanation that has stood the test of time focuses on the collapse of the U.S. banking system and resulting contraction of the nation's money stock. Economists Milton Friedman and Anna Schwartz make a strong case that a falling money stock caused the sharp decline in output and prices in the economy.[2]

As the money stock fell, spending on goods and services declined, which in turn caused firms to cut prices and output and to lay off workers. The resulting decline in incomes made it harder for borrowers to repay loans. Defaults and bankruptcies soared, creating a vicious spiral in which more banks failed, the money stock contracted further, and output, prices and employment continued to decline.[3]

## MONEY, BANKING AND DEFLATION

Money makes the economy function. Money evolved thousands of years ago because barter—the direct trading of goods or services for other goods or services— simply didn't work. A modern economy could not function without money, and economies tend to break down when the quantity or value of money changes suddenly or dramatically. Print too much money, and its value declines—that is, prices rise (inflation). Shrink the money stock, on the other hand, and the value of money rises— that is, prices fall (deflation).

In modern economies, bank deposits—not coins or currency—comprise the lion's share of the money stock. Bank deposits are created when banks make loans, and deposits contract when customers repay loans. The amount of loans that banks can make, and hence the quantity of deposits that are created, is determined partly by regulations on the amount of reserves that banks must hold against their deposits and partly by the business judgment of bankers.

In the United States, bank reserves consist of the cash that banks hold in their vaults and the deposits they keep at Federal Reserve banks. Reserves earn little or no interest, so banks don't like to hold too much of them.
On the other hand, if banks hold too few reserves, they risk getting caught short in the event of unexpected deposit withdrawals.

In the 1930s, the United States was on the gold standard, meaning that the U.S. government would exchange dollars for gold at a fixed price. Commercial banks, as well as Federal Reserve banks, held a portion of their reserves in the form of gold coin and bullion, as required by law.

An increase in gold reserves, which might come from domestic mining or inflows of gold from abroad, would enable banks to increase their lending and, as a result, would tend to inflate the money stock. A decrease in reserves, on the other hand, would tend to contract the money stock. For example, large withdrawals of cash or gold from banks could reduce bank reserves to the point that banks would have to contract their outstanding loans, which would further reduce deposits and shrink the money stock.

The money stock fell during the Great Depression primarily because of banking panics. Banking systems rely on the confidence of depositors that they will be able to access their funds in banks whenever they need them. If that confidence is shaken—perhaps by the failure of an important bank or large commercial firm—people will rush to withdraw their deposits to avoid losing their funds if their own bank fails.

Because banks hold only a fraction of the value of their customers' deposits in the form of reserves, a sudden, unexpected attempt to convert deposits into cash can leave banks short of reserves. Ordinarily, banks can borrow extra reserves from other banks or from the Federal Reserve. However, borrowing from other banks becomes extremely expensive or even impossible when depositors make demands on all banks. During the Great Depression, many banks could not or would not borrow from the Federal Reserve because they either lacked acceptable collateral or did not belong to the Federal Reserve System.[4]

Starting in 1930, a series of banking panics rocked the U.S. financial system. As depositors pulled funds out of banks, banks lost reserves and had to contract their loans and deposits, which reduced the nation's money stock. The monetary contraction, as well as the financial chaos associated with the failure of large numbers of banks, caused the economy to collapse.

Less money and increased borrowing costs reduced spending on goods and services, which caused firms to cut back on production, cut prices and lay off workers. Falling prices and incomes, in turn, led to even more economic distress. Deflation increased the real burden of debt and left many firms and households with too little income to repay their loans. Bankruptcies and defaults increased, which caused thousands of banks to fail. In each year from 1930 to 1933, more than 1,000 U.S. banks closed.

Banking panics are pretty much a thing of the past, thanks to federal deposit insurance. Widespread failures of banks and savings institutions during the 1980s did not cause depositors to panic, which limited withdrawals from the banking system and prevented serious reverberations throughout the economy. Similarly, banks did not face large-scale deposit withdrawals during the financial crisis of 2007-09. However, investors lost confidence in money market mutual funds, prompting a temporary federal guarantee of those funds to slow withdrawals. Also, many banks and other financial firms were unable to roll over their short-term debt in wholesale funding markets, forcing a few of them out of business.

**David C. Wheelock is a vice president and deputy director of research at the Federal Reserve Bank of St. Louis.**

1. In 1929, federal net outlays totaled $3.1 billion and GDP totaled $104.6 billion. In 1939, federal net outlays totaled $9.1 billion and GDP totaled $93.5 billion. Data are from Federal Reserve Economic Data (FRED®), Federal Reserve Bank of St. Louis.
   http://research.stlouisfed.org/fred2/series/FYONET
   http://research.stlouisfed.org/fred2/series/GDPA

2. Milton Friedman and Anna J. Schwartz. *A Monetary History of the United States, 1867-1960.* Princeton: Princeton University Press, 1963.

3. Former Federal Reserve Chairman Ben Bernanke wrote an important article showing that banking panics contributed to the nation's economic collapse not only by reducing the money stock, but also by increasing the costs of borrowing and lending. Ben S. Bernanke. "Nonmonetary Effects of the Financial Crisis in Propagation of the Great Depression," *American Economic Review*, June 1983, v. 73, issue 3, pp. 257-76.

4. Before 1980, only banks that were members of the Federal Reserve System could borrow directly from Federal Reserve banks.

inflation year over year. Ask them what they notice about real GDP growth during recessions (as indicated by a shaded area on the graph) and what they notice about percent change in inflation during recessions. Ask students what the graphs show for the period between 1929 and 1939—deflation (or negative inflation), unemployment as high as 25%, and declining real GDP. Ask students to explain what these data communicate about the time period.

### Dimension 3: Evaluating Sources and Using Evidence

Successful inquiry requires that students "Gather relevant information from multiple sources representing a wide range of views while using the origin, authority, structure, context, and corroborative value of the sources to guide the selection." (D3.1.9-12) To accomplish this goal, have students explore additional source material regarding the Great Depression found in Federal Reserve Archival System for Economic Research (FRASER), http://fraser.stlouisfed.org. These sources may require scaffolds for students to make meaningful use of them. Consider using historical source scaffolds such as APARTS or SCIM-C. These scaffolds are designed to support students as they conduct document analysis. You may also need to excerpt material from these sources, depending on the time available.

Have students evaluate information from the various sources with regard to the value of that information in responding to the compelling question framing the inquiry. Based on the content learned from various sources students should take a position on an issue arising from the compelling question, "Why Do We Call It The 'Great' Depression?" For example, a position might be that another recession of the magnitude of the Great Depression can be avoided. Or, students might provide an explanation for why the Great Depression lasted so long, and so on.

Have students create a fishbone diagram illustrating the causes and effects of the Great Depression. To create the Fishbone (or Ishikawa) diagram, students should decide on one major effect that relates to the compelling question, Why Do We Call It The "Great" Depression? For example, they might select "Great Depression" as the effect. This effect should be placed in the head of the diagram. Then, students should then start thinking about causes. They should list causes on the bones of the fish and try to arrange these causes in categories so that patterns can be determined.

Have students annotate the diagram indicating sources that support their claims. Point out that students should use data to explain why this was a "Great Depression," describing the magnitude of change and the duration of change.

Students can also review the measures that were taken (and not taken) to deal with the Great Depression. New Deal programs were carried out in two stages—from 1933-1934, and from 1935-1941. They focused on three areas:

1.  Relief programs that would help immediately (for example the Works Progress Administration, the Federal Emergency Relief Administration, and the Federal Theatre Project);

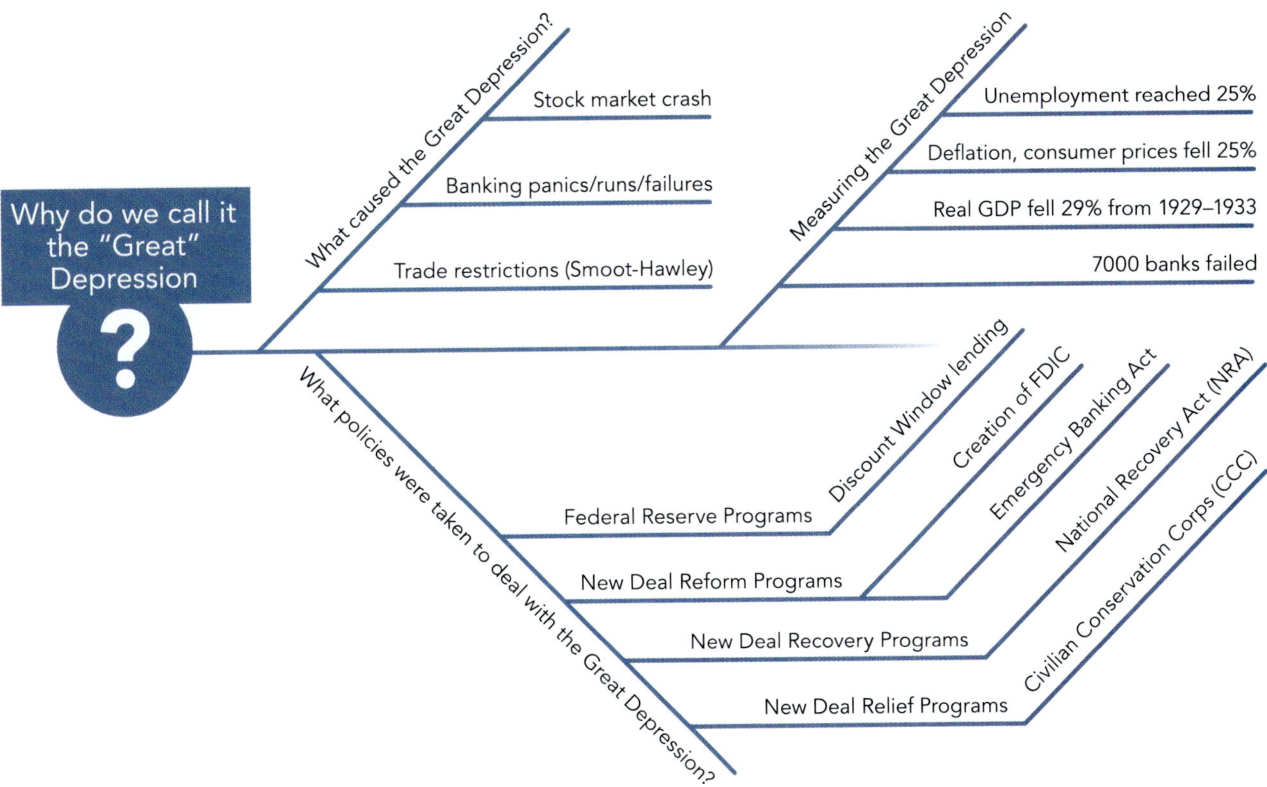


Fishbone diagram illustrating the causes and effects of the Great Depression.

2. Recovery programs that would help rebuild the economy (such as the Farm Security Administration and the Agricultural Adjustment Administration); and

3. Reform programs to prevent the disaster from recurring (such as the establishment of the Federal Deposit Insurance Corporation, known as the FDIC, which guaranteed bank deposits).

Students could consider both the extent and limitations of these initiatives. One group of students could examine relief programs and evaluate their impact. A second group could study recovery programs and appraise their effectiveness. A third group could focus on reform programs by identifying the objectives of the programs and weighing the evidence on whether or not these objectives were accomplished. Roosevelt's programs certainly restored confidence in the financial system and in the U.S. economy. However, the Great Depression went on for a very long time despite the New Deal measures, and students should also consider the possible limitations of some of the measures. For example, did the Revenue Act (Wealth Tax Act) of 1935 have a negative effect on GDP by reducing investment and incentives to produce? Did the National Recovery Act (NRA) encourage the formation of industrial cartels, limit competition, and discourage employment? Did the New Deal agricultural programs slow the economic recovery by discouraging production and employment?

Students could also examine the role of the Federal Reserve in allowing the money stock to collapse. Runs on the banks led to bank failures because banks had converted many of the deposits of customers into loans and did not have reserves to meet the demands of so many customers to withdraw their money. The Fed could have helped to solve the problem of the lack of the necessary reserves by lowering the discount interest rate, opening discount window access to more banks, and making more open market purchases of securities. The Fed learned from its mistakes and reacted very differently to the Great Recession arising from the financial crisis of 2007-2009. Students could study the options available to the Federal Reserve at different times in the Great Depression, and consider policies that might have been more effective than those actually followed in restoring confidence in the financial system and reviving the economy.

### Dimension 4: Communicating Conclusions and Taking Informed Action

In communicating their arguments regarding this Great Depression inquiry, regardless of the method of communication, students should acknowledge various views by presenting an opposing point of view and then forwarding an argument that supports their view and explains the error in the opposition's view—citing sources as evidence to do so.  Students might choose to develop an argument regarding what ended the Great Depression. In doing so, they must recognize the argument held by many that Roosevelt's New Deal programs ended the Depression. Then citing sources, they might develop support for an argument that the primary role of the New Deal programs was a change in consumer confidence and that other economic factors actually brought the Great Depression to an end.

Students should use the annotated fishbone diagram they created, data, and information from the sources they have identified to communicate their findings about the Great Depression. Provide the following suggestions for communicating results. All examples should include use of data and information from sources. All data and sources should be properly cited. The C3 Framework suggests that students should "construct explanations using sound reasoning, correct sequence (linear or non-linear), examples, and details with significant and pertinent information and data, while acknowledging the strengths and weaknesses of the explanation given its purpose (e.g., cause and effect, chronological, procedural, technical)." (D4.2.9-12) Following are examples of how students might accomplish this communication task.

#### WRITE A REPORT TO A CONGRESSIONAL COMMITTEE REGARDING THE CAUSES OF AND PROPOSALS FOR ENDING THE GREAT DEPRESSION

Such a report should indicate an understanding of the various factors that contributed to the Great Depression including decreasing money stock, bank failures, the stock market crash, deflation, and the Smoot-Hawley Tariff. Proposals for ending the Great Depression should include policies that could be undertaken by the Federal Reserve and/or the government for expanding the money stock, regenerating consumer confidence in the banking system, and promoting employment. Students should identify the impact of these potential policies on unemployment, government spending, real GDP, and consumer confidence. The report should draw on real GDP, inflation, and unemployment data for the time period. The report should include an analysis of the data based on an understanding of the factors that contributed to the Great Depression.

### USE VIDEO, OR PERHAPS AUDIO EQUIPMENT, TO RECORD A NEWS STORY PLACED DURING THE GREAT DEPRESSION (E.G. AN OLD TIME NEWS REEL OR RADIO PROGRAM). THE VIDEO OR RADIO PROGRAM SHOULD INCLUDE INTERVIEWS WITH FICTIONAL PEOPLE (POLICY MAKERS AND CITIZENS) WHO LIVED DURING THE PERIOD.

Videos or audio recordings should include information from citizens who were affected by the stock market crash, unemployment, deflation, and bank failures, sharing their stories. Policy makers should suggest policies that could be undertaken by the Federal Reserve and/or the federal government and explain how these policies would affect unemployment, government spending, real GDP and consumer confidence to alleviate citizens' distress. Either the interviewer or the policy maker should draw on relevant data.

### PRODUCE A DOCUMENTARY THAT EXPLORES ONE OR MORE OF THE QUESTIONS DEVELOPED DURING THE INQUIRY STAGE OF THE LESSON.

The documentary should employ graphs and charts that indicate an understanding of economic indicators—real GDP, unemployment, and inflation. In addition, depending on the question, the documentary should address the factors that together created the worst economic collapse in U.S. history, and address the impact of New Deal policies, the failure of the Federal Reserve to act appropriately, and so on.

### COMPARE A RECENT RECESSION TO THE GREAT DEPRESSION. WHAT SIMILARITIES AND DIFFERENCES ARE EVIDENT? WRITE AN ESSAY EXPLAINING THE ANALYSIS.

The essay should compare the primary economic indicators related to recessions between the two events—real GDP growth, unemployment rates, and the duration of the two events. In addition, the essay should compare factors that led to/created the problem as well as a comparison of the Fed's monetary policy actions and the federal government's fiscal policy actions relative to the two events.

# About the Federal Reserve Bank of St. Louis

The Federal Reserve Bank of St. Louis is one of 12 Federal Reserve Banks in the Federal Reserve System. The Federal Reserve Bank of St. Louis is the 8th District of the Federal Reserve System serving parts of Missouri, Illinois, Indiana, Kentucky, Tennessee and all of Arkansas. As part of its outreach efforts, the Federal Reserve Bank of St. Louis provides online resources—courses, videos, podcasts, lesson plans, and whiteboard activities to K-12 educators throughout the country, free of charge.

*The authors of this chapter are Mary Suiter, assistant vice president and economic education officer at the Federal Reserve Bank of St. Louis; Barbara Flowers, economic education coordinator at the Federal Reserve Bank of St. Louis; and Scott Wolla, senior economic education specialist at the Federal Reserve Bank of St. Louis. The opinions expressed in this chapter are those of the authors and not those of the Federal Reserve Bank of St. Louis or the Federal Reserve System.*

CHAPTER 11

# What **Don't** You Know About Civil Rights?

**Newseum**

Freedom Summer Training Sessions at Western College for Women in Oxford, Ohio, during the first of two week-long sessions held there in June 1964. Volunteers stand beside their bus, hand-in-hand, singing together before leaving for Mississippi to help blacks register to vote.

TED POLUMBAUM/NEWSEUM COLLECTION

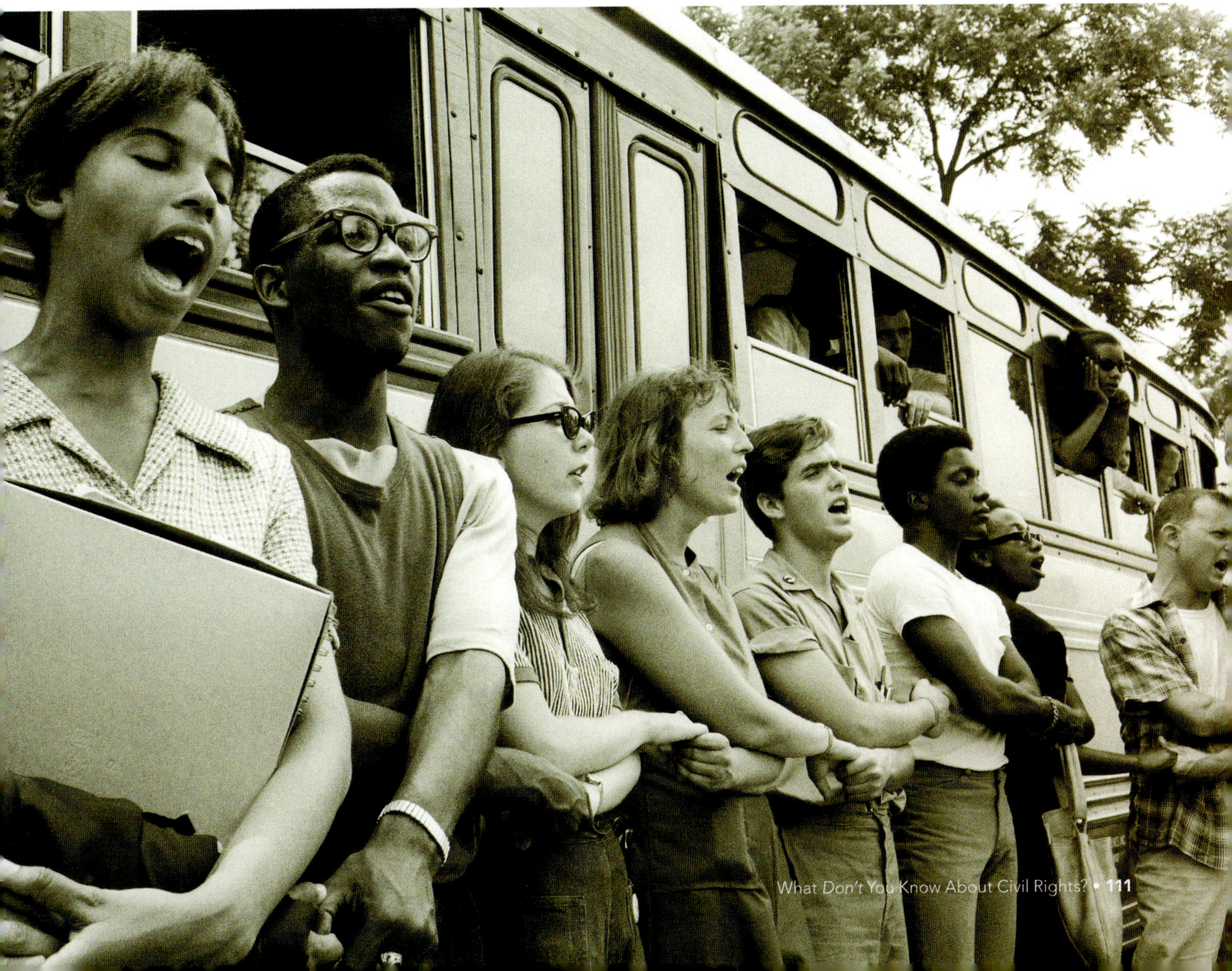

### Newseum Education Department

| C3 Disciplinary Focus | C3 Inquiry Focus | Content Topic |
|---|---|---|
| U.S. History, Civics | Developing questions, evaluating sources, and communicating conclusions | The civil rights movement |

**C3 Focus Indicators**

**D1:** Explain how a question represents key ideas in the field. (D1.1.6-8)

**D2:** Explain multiple causes and effects of events and developments in the past. (D2.His.14.6-8)

**D3:** Identify evidence that draws information from multiple sources to support claims, noting evidentiary limitations. (D3.3.6-8)

**D3:** Develop claims and counterclaims while pointing out the strengths and limitations of both. (D3.4.6-8)

**D4:** Present adaptations of arguments and explanations on topics of interest to others to reach audiences and venues outside the classroom using print and oral technologies. (D4.3.6-8)

| Grade Level | Resources | Time Required |
|---|---|---|
| 6–8 | Resources cited in chapter; the Newseum Digital Classroom website | 3 class periods |

# Introduction and Connections to the C3 Framework

Ask your students what they know about the civil rights movement, and they'll probably fire back a volley of marquee names, milestone events and bumper-sticker quotes: "I Have a Dream!" "Martin Luther King Jr.!" "The March on Washington!" "Rosa Parks!" Ask your students what they don't know about the civil rights movement, and you'll probably get an awkward silence punctuated by the odd "Huh?" or "What?"

How can you help your students move beyond the checklist of civil rights facts and figures toward a deeper understanding of the factors that shaped the civil rights movement and an appreciation for its continuing impact in their own communities and around the world? How can you help them step away from their instinct for easy answers to instead begin formulating and investigating their own questions?

This chapter explores how you can reframe the civil rights movement using the four dimensions of the C3 Framework and the Newseum's emphasis on the role of the First Amendment, with special attention to the power of the free press and its reporting of the "first draft of history." Together, these conceptual tools can help trigger your students' realization that while their knowledge of civil rights basics provides an essential foundation, identifying, embracing, and investigating what they don't know about the movement can prove even more fruitful. The result: students are empowered to direct their learning process, while increasing their content knowledge about the civil rights movement.

The instructional ideas spelled out below build on the Making a Change civil rights learning module, a free interactive resource on the Newseum Digital Classroom. The module uses the First Amendment as a lens to present familiar faces and events in new ways, shining light on often-overlooked aspects of the movement. Some of the content—such as dramatic juxtapositions of Northern and Southern front pages covering *Brown v. Board of Education* or a student newsletter produced by a Mississippi "Freedom School" during Freedom Summer—may surprise and even shock students who've mainly been exposed to the more simplified accounts of that era.

The ideas laid out in this chapter leverage that shock and surprise to propel the C3 Inquiry Arc. Students first practice crafting compelling and supporting questions about the civil rights movement. Then they think historically to make claims about turning points in the movement, while also applying multidisciplinary concepts from geography and civics; use evidence from the module's wealth of primary sources to support their arguments; and finally share, debate, and act on their findings about the civil rights movement and its local and global connections.

NEWSEUM COLLECTION

# Inquiry Arc

The combination of the Newseum's civil rights content and the C3 Framework presents an opportunity for students to discover what they don't know about the civil rights movement and its continuing legacy, and go in search of new knowledge. Using the resources of the Newseum Digital Classroom, this lesson traverses the four dimensions of the C3 inquiry arc in a few class periods, with a special emphasis on Dimension 1: questioning. The end goal of these instructional ideas is the fostering of a community of learners that extends beyond a single classroom. Such a community revels in meaty questions, knows how to work toward nuanced answers, and communicates its findings in ways that inspire ongoing conversations about the past, present, and future of the First Amendment and its impact on the civil rights movement.

## Dimension 1: Developing Questions and Planning Inquiries

At the Newseum, we call them the "reporter's questions," but students may know them as the "5 W's and an H": who, what, where, when, why, and how. They may be simple, but these six basic questions are a helpful starting point for creating supporting and compelling questions.

Helping students learn to create their own compelling questions is one of the biggest challenges of implementing the C3 Framework. Students may not be accustomed to focusing on what they don't know. So before delving into what students *don't* know about the civil rights movement and forming questions to fill those holes, gather what they *do* know. Work as a class to fill out a chart of their existing knowledge of the movement:

- Who participated?
- Where did its major events take place?
- When did its major events take place?
- Why was it needed?
- How did it operate/achieve its goals?
- What impact did it have?

Depending on your students' familiarity with the topic, you can send them to explore the Protesting for Right civil rights timeline on the Making a Change module either as a refresher before embarking on your chart or to gather more specifics after a first round of filling in information.

Once you've exhausted student knowledge, find the reporter's question with the fewest answers, and work as a class to craft additional questions that could help uncover more information. Remind your students that they don't need to know the answers to the questions they're generating—they just need to be curious about the answers. It may be helpful to send them back to the timeline to look for inspiration. Their first ideas may be narrow or specific, and are more likely to be supporting questions (e.g., Who else, besides Martin Luther King Jr., spoke at the March on Washington? How did the movement's participants get the word out about upcoming protests?) than compelling questions. This is an important first step toward envisioning a broader inquiry.

Once you've brainstormed a dozen or more of these types of questions, ask your students to consider them all together and start looking for themes. Work with your students to group multiple smaller questions into one bigger question. If your conversation loses momentum, you can return to the Newseum's resources to enliven the conversation and focus students' attention on compelling questions that historians may consider when examining this movement. Students might develop questions such as these: How would the March on Washington have been different if there were no freedom of speech? What role did the free press play in keeping both observers and participants informed about the movement? How has the First Amendment fundamentally shaped our nation's history?

You can also begin to structure students' ideas by using the concept of historical turning points.

At the Newseum, we've found historical turning points—those moments often captured in the most dramatic newsreels, front pages, and tweets—to be a concept ripe for deeper exploration, with connections to skills and concepts from multiple disciplines, but simple enough to draw in learners at many different levels. The story of the civil rights movement can be told as a series of turning points, and using this concept along with historical sources in the Making a Change module connects history, geography, economics, and civics.

Turning points can help generate compelling questions. For example, was *Brown v. Board of Education* a turning point in history? That's a compelling question in and of itself. The question is open ended, requiring evidence, and certainly worthy of investigation. Keep in mind that the first indicator in Dimension 1 of the C3 Framework asks students to "explain how a compelling question represents key ideas in the field." (D1.1.6-8) As students develop their questions, facilitate their reflection on the importance of those questions!

Turning points are not only an historical concept. The Making a Change module emphasizes geography by presenting front pages reporting on six milestone civil rights events—each one arguably a turning point—from different cities around the country. Compare and contrast the historical news coverage of the civil rights movement with your students and start forming questions about how where something is published and its spatial relationship to a major event might shape its presentation of that event.

There are also ties to civics. Turning points aren't a product of spontaneous combustion—people spark and shape these events. In the context of the civil rights movement, people exercising their First Amendment rights in a strategic and persistent manner changed laws and shifted social mores—but not without resistance. Asking questions about what it takes to make a turning point is a great introduction to the potential power of engaged citizens to affect their nation.

Think of this question-building process as climbing an inverted pyramid. Start with the small, simple reporter's questions; build to bigger but still specific supporting questions; then finally look for the broad themes that support thick, compelling questions. The First Amendment and turning points can be stepping stools to help students move up the pyramid. Depending on your students' questioning skills, they may or may not make it all the way to robust compelling questions on their own. That's where you can step in to guide their ideas, layering and shaping them to spring into the next three dimensions of the C3 inquiry arc.

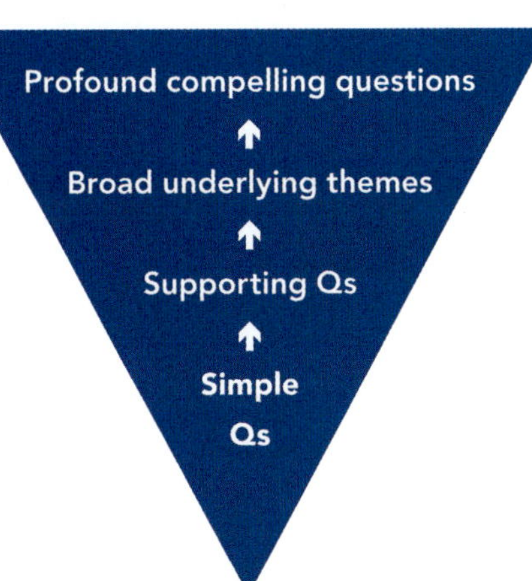


## Dimension 2: Connections to Disciplinary Tools and Concepts

Although there is no universal definition, a turning point can be simply explained as an event or set of events that, had it unfolded differently, would have changed the way history played out. In other words, it's an event with an impact that shapes the events to follow. Historians view turning points as important markers of cause and effect. The C3

Framework also emphasizes cause and effect, expecting students to "explain multiple causes and effects of events and developments in the past." (D2.His.14.6-8)

The inquiry arc structure of the C3 Framework suggests that students can examine cause and effect after they pose a question and before they analyze sources, but incorporating Dimension 2 into your students' inquiries cannot and should not be strictly linear. Students will need to use the skills and concepts featured in Dimension 2 throughout their inquiries, from initial questioning to communicating their findings. However, it is also important to stop and emphasize certain concepts and skills. You might think of this as digging a posthole along the way in building a fence. As you support students in their inquiry, it's a good idea periodically to stop and dig a posthole by going in depth with targeted content from Dimension 2. This fosters students' development of knowledge and skills from the social studies disciplines.

The Supreme Court ruling in *Brown v. Board of Education,* an important civil rights turning point, provides a posthole opportunity to explore historical cause and effect. The Making a Change module's media map, found under the module's Media Literacy tab, includes front pages from newspapers across the country that were published in the days and months after the 1954 *Brown v. Board* decision. Students can read these articles from the *Topeka State Journal, Jackson Daily News, Providence Journal, Chicago American,* and *Cleveland News* to gain some insight into the causes and effects of the decision. To initiate this activity, have students make some preliminary statements about what caused the *Brown v. Board* plaintiffs to sue their school districts and what caused the Supreme Court to take up the case. In groups, have students read the *Brown v. Board* coverage on one of the five front pages on the Media Map. To supplement students' understanding, you might also have them read the syllabus from the actual *Brown v. Board* decision, available online from the Oyez Project (http://www.oyez.org). Then, discuss as a class how the facts they've gathered align with their initial thoughts on the causes of the case and catalog the effects it triggered, both short- and long-term. Guide students to focus on concrete connections, citing evidence from their front-page research whenever possible. More advanced students may also begin to examine the interplay between multiple causes and effects and how the press shaped both the lead-up to and impacts of the event. This analysis should lead to students being able to explain why the *Brown v. Board of Education* decision was a turning point in history.

### Dimension 3: Evaluating Sources and Using Evidence

As students formulate their own ideas in response to their compelling questions, these ideas will take the form of claims. Beginning as early as third grade, Dimension 3 expects that students will "use evidence to develop claims in response to compelling questions." (D3.4.3-5) In grades 6-8, students should "develop claims and counterclaims while pointing out the strengths and limitations of both." (D3.4.6-8) Getting students to make claims toward answering their question sets up a frame of reference for their investigation and reinforces the idea that history is inseparable from its practitioners' perspectives and interpretations.

# What were the consequences of the *Brown v. Board of Education* (1954) ruling?

**1951:** Striking students in Farmville, Va., protest substandard school building.

COURTESY HANK WALKER/TIME & LIFE PICTURES/GETTY IMAGES

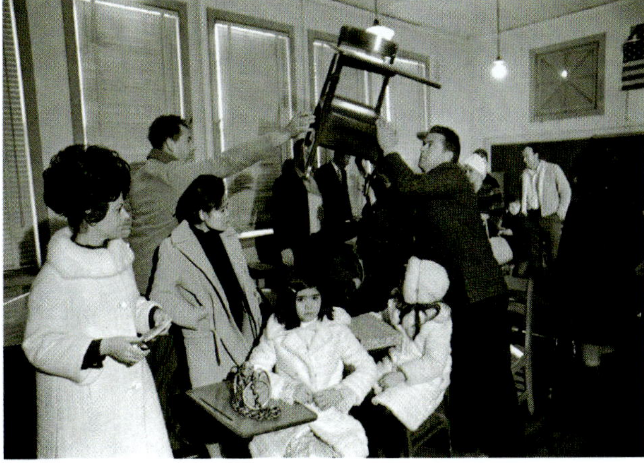

**1969:** Parents staging a sit-in to protest their children being sent to a formerly all-black middle school.

CONSTANCE W. CURRY PAPERS, MANUSCRIPT, ARCHIVES AND RARE BOOKS LIBRARY, ROBERT W. WOODFRUFF LIBRARY, EMORY UNIVERSITY

Students will be holding up their claims against others to compare and contrast their ideas with peers' and experts' findings and opinions. As they adjust and strengthen their claims, students bring together information they have gathered from historical sources as evidence.

Returning to the school desegregation topic we introduced earlier, the Newseum Digital Classroom offers a rich collection of sources to support students in developing claims and using evidence on questions related to this topic. Below is a sample of the potential evidence available within the Protesting for Right timeline to support inquiry about *Brown v. Board* or other civil rights turning points.

Imagine a student starting from a claim that *Brown v. Board* was a turning point because it united black and white students across the nation and allowed black students to obtain a higher quality education. That student might zero in on the photograph of the substandard school building that prompted students in Farmville, Va., to strike in 1951. She could find the newspaper article reporting on the Brown decision, stating the clear implication that black students would be allowed to attend white schools, but with no specific deadline for this change. She might also find the photograph of white parents staging a sit-in in 1969 to protest sending their children to a formerly all-black middle school. This evidence shows that *Brown v. Board* changed things, but not immediately and not universally. Time to amend that initial claim!

As part of this process, students should carefully analyze the sources they are citing, whether they are primary or secondary. To help with this process, the Newseum turns back to the trusty reporter's questions. But this time, we turn them around into the "consumer's questions"—questions that people consuming information should ask about their sources:

**CONSUMER'S QUESTIONS**

- Who made this?
- How was it made?
- Why was it made?
- When was this made?

- What information is missing?
- Where do I go from here to find more information?

These questions will support students as they develop skills highlighted in the C3 Framework, specifically that students will "evaluate the credibility of a source by determining its relevance and intended use." (D3.2.6-8)

### Dimension 4: Communicating Conclusions and Taking Informed Action

When the time comes to organize the information gathered, communicate conclusions, and even take action, teachers can follow many different paths, according to their instructional time and students' abilities. Below, listed roughly in order of increasing time and resource commitment, are a few ideas for Dimension 4 assessments to cap this exploration of the civil rights movement. All provide the opportunity to apply civic virtues and democratic principles through collaborative work and discourse. The activities described below align with the C3 Framework and will help students develop the skills to "present adaptations of arguments and explanations on topics of interest to others to reach audiences and venues outside the classroom using print and oral technologies." (D4.3.6-8)

#### CREATE A NEWS REPORT

What would news coverage of these events look like if they happened today? How would you avoid the bias evidenced by some historical news sources? Using the information gathered during their investigation, have students create a news report about their turning point and its impact using a modern medium—a blog, Twitter stream, etc. Share and critique the reports as a class. (In the Newseum Digital Classroom Making a Change module, Media Literacy Lesson Plan 2 offers supporting materials.)

#### MAKE A CLASS MAP

Which issues that the civil rights movement addressed remain the targets of protest in the U.S. and beyond? What is the global status of equal access to education? Fair wage movements? Voting rights? Students can explore whether the changes their turning points put in motion have had lasting impact in the U.S. and look domestically and internationally for places where these types of changes have yet to be made. Use their findings to make a class map, physical or virtual, with pins marking "hot spots" for ongoing civil rights battles. Analyze any patterns that emerge.

#### INTEGRATE LOCAL CIVIL RIGHTS HISTORY

How did the civil rights movement affect your community? Were there protests? Who was involved? What happened? Have students apply the skills they practiced over the course of this inquiry arc to investigate local civil rights history with the help of parents, neighbors or a local historical society. Once they've identified a key local civil rights event, they can prepare text and multimedia resources to submit for potential inclusion in the Protesting for Right timeline. (In the Newseum Digital Classroom Making a Change module, Historical Connections Lesson Plan 3 offers supporting materials.)

Taking inspiration from the goals, methods, and impact of the civil rights movement, make a plan to address a current issue in your community. Lead your students through a service learning experience, from identifying and understanding an issue to creating a plan to taking action—or zoom in on a single part of the process. Document their work and share it on the Newseum Digital Classroom Making a Change module, using the GlogsterEDU tool to create multimedia panels for our online exhibit about contemporary civil rights issues. (See the Making a Change Civics and Citizenship Lesson Plans 1, 2, and 3 for supporting materials.)

# About the Newseum

The mission of the Newseum is to champion the five freedoms of the First Amendment through education, information, and entertainment. One of the top attractions in Washington, D.C., the Newseum's 250,000-square-foot news museum offers visitors a state-of-the-art experience that blends news history with up-to-the-second technology and hands-on exhibits.

The Newseum Institute is committed to the civic education of the public as a means of preserving our First Amendment liberties. Newseum Education, as part of the Institute, serves teachers and students around the country by connecting museum content and thought leadership to classroom goals, with an emphasis on providing dynamic resources that support student inquiry, investigation, and discourse. Educational offerings— including workshops, lesson plans, and online resources—cover topics ranging from the Civil War to civil rights, from the rights and responsibilities of the free press to freedom of speech in schools.

For additional materials and resources to support this lesson, please visit the following URLs:

- Newseum Digital Classroom, Making a Change module:
  http://newseumdigitalclassroom.org/digital-classroom/modules/civil-rights/default.aspx
  The Making a Change module is endorsed by National Council for the Social Studies.
- Newseum website: http://www.newseum.org/
- Newseum Education website: http://newseum.org/education/

*This lesson was created by the Newseum Education Department. Its author is curriculum developer Kirsti Kenneth. Anna Kassinger, multimedia curriculum specialist at the Newseum, provided special assistance.*

# CHAPTER 12

# How Can Rivers Be Managed to **Decrease Conflict** Between Groups?

**National Geographic Society**

AUDREY KREMER FOR THE NATIONAL GEOGRAPHIC SOCIETY, 2006

**National Geographic Education**

| **C3 Disciplinary Focus** | **C3 Inquiry Focus** | **Content Topic** |
|---|---|---|
| Geography | Using disciplinary concepts to evaluate evidence and construct arguments | Conflict over river resources |

**C3 Focus Indicators**

**D1:** Explain how the relationship between supporting questions and compelling questions is mutually reinforcing. (D1.4.6-8)

**D2:** Use maps, satellite images, photographs, and other representations to explain relationships between the locations of places and regions, and changes in their environmental characteristics. (D2.Geo.2.6-8)

**D3:** Evaluate the credibility of a source by determining its relevance and intended use. (D3.2.6-8)

**D4:** Construct arguments using claims and evidence from multiple sources, while acknowledging the strengths and limitations of the arguments. (D4.1.6-8)

*This lesson can also be adapted for use in Grades 9-12 to achieve the comparable C3 objectives for that grade level.*

| **Grade Level** | **Resources** | **Time Required** |
|---|---|---|
| 6–8 and higher | Resources cited in chapter; National Geographic Education website | 2–4 class periods |

# Introduction and Connections to the C3 Framework

Geography is defined as a study of places and the relationships between people and their environments. Geography seeks to understand where things are found, why they are there, and how they develop and change over time. Yet equipping today's students with the skills, knowledge, and perspectives they need to be responsible and effective citizens calls for educational experiences that go beyond "knowing" geography to "doing" geography.

> The goal of teaching geography is to equip students with the knowledge, skills, and perspectives to "do" geography. Reaching this goal requires that students learn how to use geographic thinking and information to make well-reasoned decisions and to solve personal and community problems. Many valuable applications of K-12 geography education lie beyond the classroom walls. Geographic education enables students to use geographic perspectives, knowledge, and skills to engage in ethical action with regard to self, other people, other species, and Earth's diverse cultures and natural environments. Geography connects students to world events, problems, and decisions throughout their lives.*
>
> — **Geography For Life: National Geography Standards, Second Edition**

The ideas presented in this chapter provide teachers with tools to support sound geographic education—encompassing students' understanding of the complex world and their roles in it. Through a scenario involving conflict over rights to river resources, students frame supporting questions from a teacher-generated compelling question. Then, they analyze the key issues and stakeholder perspectives impacting the critical decisions in a conflict and formulate conclusions that they share and evaluate with their peers. Finally, they identify a current issue related to a conflict over rivers and follow an inquiry path that culminates in students explaining the issue and presenting their conclusions.

This chapter offers two options regarding content for investigation. You can use a case or topic that relates to your community or curriculum or you can use the case in "Conflict on the Danube," a lesson available in the National Geographic unit, *Beyond Borders* (see pages 126–127), for which further information is available on the National Geographic Education website. The overall theme of this teacher-tested unit is using maps to understand borders and their impacts in Europe. The materials are designed to help middle school students use maps to think about how borders intersect physical and human geographical features and how those intersections can lead to cooperation and/or conflict. They can also be used, with suitable modifications, at the high school level.

* S. Heffron and R. Downs, eds., *Geography for Life: National Geography Standards*, Second Edition (Washington, DC: Geography Education National Implementation Project, 2012). The text quoted is on the copyright page of the book.

# Inquiry Arc

## Dimension 1: Developing Questions and Planning Inquiries

A key component for inquiry in all disciplines is the framing of compelling questions; however, it is a skill that is difficult for students of any age. Depending on your students' prior knowledge or familiarity with questioning skills, it is important to begin with an activity on developing good questions. To set the stage for the activities to come, what follows is a scenario of conflicts over rivers.

**POSE THE FOLLOWING SCENARIO TO STUDENTS:**



Ask students what they know about the river and the situation from this scenario. Take responses from students until you're confident the main points of the issue are understood.

Then write the following question on the board: *How can rivers be managed to decrease conflict and increase cooperation between groups?* Tell students that this is an example of a compelling question—a question that addresses big ideas about an issue or concept. Explain that a compelling question is a broad and interesting question that makes you want to learn more—to ask more questions.

Ask students to work in small groups to locate a specific river that is relevant given your teaching needs. You might use the Danube River and study the conflict over "Rivers and the Gabčíkovo-Nagymaros Project" content (see page 127). Students should customize the compelling question, given the river they identified. For example, if they are focusing on the "Rivers and the Gabčíkovo-Nagymaros Project" the resulting compelling question could be, How can the Danube river be managed to decrease conflict and increase cooperation between groups?

Compelling questions cannot be answered easily; they need supporting questions to provide direction for further investigation. Supporting questions help students get more information to answer the compelling question. Students may need some examples of good supporting questions. Some supporting questions that follow from the scenario above might include, How do Community A and Community B compare in size? How might the size of the communities impact the conflict? What impact does the upstream dam have on the river and the resources it provides? What does it mean to "manage" a river?

When discussing issues related to rights, students at the middle school level will often bring up concepts of fairness and sharing things equally. They may not think about the different factors that can impact the situation, such as community sizes, other sources of water for the community, or environmental impacts. Prompt students to think about some of these factors, especially if they are having trouble coming up with questions. Remind students that good supporting questions will not be "yes" or "no" questions or questions that encourage short or single-word answers; they will be open-ended questions that require more thinking and some research.

It is important for students to recognize that, as stated in C3 Indicator D1.4.6-8, compelling and supporting questions reinforce one another. The compelling question informs the inquiry and leads to supporting questions that address what students need to find out. The supporting questions are built from and refer back to the compelling question and make it possible to seek and find answers to the compelling question.

Explain to students that in this activity they have identified some questions about key ideas in geography. As you transition into the next activity, tell students that they will explore concepts related to conflict over rivers. Ask students to keep their compelling question in mind as they work through the next activity.

## Dimension 2: Connections to Disciplinary Tools and Concepts

Building geographic skills around key ideas in the discipline is critical to developing geo-literate students. The use of maps and other representations helps students explain the interconnections and relationships between places, regions, the physical features of places, and the people who live there. (C3 Indicator D2.Geo.2.6-8) Using a large map that features rivers, ask students to identify physical features they see. Have them name the rivers they see on the map. Ask: Why are rivers important physical features? What is the role of rivers in determining borders? Brainstorm possible reasons for rivers to be a source of conflict between nations. List students' ideas and use the list to discuss positive and negative aspects of sharing resources like rivers.

# Conflict on the Danube

Provide students with copies of the Gabčíkovo-Nagymaros Project information on page 127 and have them locate maps of the region. Have students read the passage independently or in pairs, noting unfamiliar words in the reading or questions they have. As they read, students should refer to the maps to identify the locations, borders, and drainage basins mentioned. Make sure all students have a good understanding of the concepts presented in the reading—the chronology of events in the dam conflict, the positions of the countries impacted by the project and resulting conflict, and the environmental impact of the project before moving on.

- Divide the class into small groups and have each group work together to discuss and answer the following questions.
- Locate the area of the Gabčíkovo-Nagymaros Project on a map of the Danube River including the Gabčíkovo Dam. Which countries are upstream of the project? Which countries are downstream?
- The Gabčíkovo Dam and diversion canal moved more than 80 percent of the water from the Danube River out of its original course. How would this affect the people living along the original course of the river?

Have students take on the roles of stakeholders in the Gabčíkovo-Nagymaros conflict. Assign each group only one of the questions below. Tell students that their goal is to attempt to solve the conflict and to present their point of view to the International Court of Justice (the class). If possible, have students conduct additional research on the dam and its impacts before they present their answers, including creating a chart of positive versus negative effects on the aspect of the dam they explored. Have a volunteer from each group present the group's ideas to the class, supporting the ideas with facts from the reading. Allow time for classmates to ask the presenting group questions and for the presenting group to defend and/or debate their position.

1. Imagine it is 1977. You are the Hungarian and Czechoslovakian negotiators who agreed on the Gabčíkovo-Nagymaros Project. Why will this project help improve life in your countries, and why is it an example of international cooperation that other countries should follow? Include an explanation of the physical geography and the economic and political situation of the area.

2. Imagine you are representatives of Germany, Bulgaria, and Romania—three other countries along the Danube River. What are your concerns about this project? Are you in favor or opposed? What practical solutions can you suggest?

3. Imagine yourself in the role of an international environmental organization. You want to represent the rights of nature— the plants and animals living in and around the Danube. If you don't take human considerations into account, how does the way you look at the problem change? What do you suggest as the best solution?

Engage students at this point in a discussion of how the general compelling question (How can rivers be managed to decrease conflict and increase cooperation between groups?) applies to investigation of their conflict.

Your discussion should lead students to recognize that rivers are often sources of conflict, whether that conflict revolves around issues of rights to the river's resources, the role of rivers as borders, concerns over environmental impacts of activities taking place on or near rivers, or any number of other issues.

This discussion will help students as they transition to research on the conflict they identified in their compelling question.

# A River in Conflict: Rivers and the Gabčíkovo-Nagymaros Project

Rivers meet a variety of human needs: freshwater for drinking, hydroelectricity to power factories and homes, irrigation for crops, transportation for freight and people, and habitats for plants and animals. Rivers also often mark borders between countries. This can lead to power struggles between neighboring countries that both want to control a river for economic, environmental, and political reasons.

The Danube River forms part of the border between the countries of Slovakia and Hungary. This river is an example of the complications and conflicts that occur when countries share a river. The source of the Danube is in the mountains of Germany. Its size alone makes the Danube River vital to the ecology and economy of Central Europe.

The area along the border between Slovakia and Hungary is a large floodplain—an ecosystem full of biological diversity, where frequent flooding washes nutrient-rich silt over the land, feeding forests and cropland, and serving as a feeding and resting place for migratory birds. The wetlands are critical because they serve as natural filters, cleaning pollution from upstream out of the water.

Part of the floodplain between Hungary and Slovakia is called Szigetköz. This area is home to small farms, forests, and about 5,000 species of plants and animals. Underneath the area is a large freshwater reservoir that needs the filtration of the wetlands above it to keep it clean. In 1977, Hungary and what was then the country of Czechoslovakia agreed to build a system of dams and canals in the Szigetköz area. This would come to be known as the Gabčíkovo-Nagymaros Project, named for the towns at each end of the dam system. The decision to build this system of dams and canals led to a major international conflict that is still not resolved over forty years later.

In the twentieth century, many countries were searching for ways to modernize and bring electricity, industry, and a higher standard of living to their people. One of the ways they tried to improve people's lives was by harnessing rivers with large dams. This could produce hydroelectric power, provide jobs, and help stop damaging floods. These kinds of projects are still built today, but much more cautiously. It was discovered that along with electricity, jobs, and flood control came lots of environmental and political problems.

The Gabčíkovo-Nagymaros Project was agreed on in 1977. It was abandoned by the Hungarian government in the early 1980s because of worries about its environmental impact and financial problems. The Czechoslovakians finished their side of the project—the Gabčíkovo dam, or Cunova dam, in 1992. In 1993, the country of Czechoslovakia split into two: the Czech Republic and Slovakia. Slovakia took control of the area. The dam pushed more than 80 percent of the flow of the Danube out of its main riverbed and into a canal on the Slovak side of the river. This led to a huge drop in the Danube's water flow below the dam. The dam and canal system created several problems that upset the Hungarians:

- Fish populations declined as much as 80 percent due to lower water levels.
- Other animals and plants, including rare birds, have lost their natural habitat.
- Pesticides, fertilizers, and industrial pollution are concentrated and trapped behind the dam.
- The level of freshwater reservoir underneath the Szigetköz area dropped and became contaminated with the trapped pollution.
- Farmers on the Hungarian side lost access to water for irrigating their crops because the river sank to such low levels.

Hungarians were also upset about the economic impact. Slovakia received all the money from ships that used the canals and all the electricity the hydroelectric plant produced because Slovaks had built and controlled the dam and canal. Hungarians who were living in Slovakia complained they were being squeezed into a small bit of land between the canal and the old riverbed. And the Hungarian government said that, in effect, a new border was being created between the two countries that gave Slovakia more control over the river and its resources.

But Slovakia's government believed it had acted according to the original agreement between the two countries. It believed that the Hungarians' problems stemmed from the fact that they had not followed through in building the rest of the project. Slovakia's government pointed out that the Szigetköz region escaped disaster during massive flooding along the Danube in 2002 because of the flood control provided by the dams and canal.

The two countries decided to ask international organizations, including the International Court of Justice, to help them resolve their disagreement. But the countries are still in conflict after years of meetings.

Note: More resources for this activity can be found in the National Geographic lesson titled "Conflict on the Danube" at **http://www. natgeoed.org/river-conflict.**

The next step in the inquiry arc calls for students to work with sources toward formulating a conclusion or an argument. Before students begin their research, ask them to list potential types of sources they might look for. Make sure they come up with several different types, which may include news articles, journal articles, and reference material such as encyclopedia entries, websites, and infographics or data sets. Encourage students to think beyond the Internet to sources that may be available in print form in the school or public library, as well as from experts in the community. Also, make sure students gather sources that provide different perspectives on the issue.

Engage students in a discussion about what to look for in the sources. Along the way, students need to evaluate the credibility and validity of sources. (C3 Indicator D3.2.6-8) In general, students should be able to evaluate sources using questions like these:

- Who is the author or creator of the information, and is that person or group an expert in the issue or are they simply expressing an opinion without the background knowledge to support it?
- When was the information/source created? Is the information recent (in the last few years) or is it old?
- Is the information biased? Clues to bias include language that is trying to persuade rather than provide information. Make sure students understand that although they will be formulating arguments or opinions about their issue, they should look for sources that give them solid background information and are not simply opinion pieces.

You should also provide students with a few questions to help them evaluate a source's appropriateness or usefulness to their inquiry.

- What information does the source give you? Is the information in-depth enough?
- Does it provide the information you need?
- Can you understand the information? Is the language too technical or difficult to understand?
- Can you use the information in this source?

Students may tend to collect too many sources in an attempt to cover all aspects of the issue. Having too many sources may muddy the process for students, and may take students off course in their research. Encourage students to find a few really good sources that cover multiple points of view and give them the information they need to answer the questions they have formulated. It is important for students to be as focused as possible in their research, therefore making the critical evaluation of sources very important.

When you are satisfied that students have enough good sources, have them use the information to formulate conclusions about the issue. Their conclusions should provide solutions that relate to their compelling questions. Remind students that they need to support their conclusions with evidence from their research. Students need to be able to explain:

- why they think the way they do about the issue;
- what information has guided them to their conclusion;
- where they found the information, and
- why they think it is valid.

The ultimate goal is to convince the audience, in this case you and the class, that their conclusions are sound.

## Dimension 4: Communicating Conclusions and Taking Informed Action

The critical final step in the inquiry process gives students an opportunity to share their conclusions with others. There are many possible methods and media available to accomplish this, and decisions about how students will communicate conclusions depend largely on time and resources. No matter which method is used, students must present their conclusions backed up with evidence from their research (C3 Indicator D4.1.6-8). Some of the evidence can be reinforced with visual aids, if appropriate, such as simple text slides, photographs, diagrams or charts, or maps.

An interesting option is to have students draw a map of the impact areas that would help show their solutions or conclusions. The impact map would need to outline the watersheds impacted, the populations that get water from the river, the populations that use the river for recreation, the natural areas and native species that rely on the natural flow of water, and other impact areas pertinent to the issue.

Students should be prepared to answer questions during or after their presentations. They should be able to discuss the various sides to the issue they are presenting and tell why they came to their conclusions. Likewise, the class should be prepared to ask good questions—questions that call for the presenting students to clarify points and defend their conclusions, as necessary.

# About National Geographic

For over 125 years, National Geographic has explored the far reaches of the planet, unlocking its secrets and sharing them with the world. National Geographic Education, the educational outreach arm of the National Geographic Society, draws on the resources of National Geographic to create learning materials and educational experiences for young people and the adults who teach them. National Geographic Education also works to enhance the education young people receive about their interconnected world through materials development, teacher professional development, grant making and community-building activities. Information about National Geographic Education, its materials, and its programs is available at http://NatGeoEd.org.

*The authors of this article are Elaine Larson, Manager of Instructional Design, and Kathleen Schwille, Vice President, Education Design and Development, at National Geographic Education.*

# Whose Job is it to **Fix** Environmental Problems?
## Case Studies from Native America

**National Museum of the American Indian**

Mother Salmon
DRAWING COURTESY OF SI LOW LEET SA
(DORALEE SANCHEZ, LUMMI NATION)

**National Museum of the American Indian (NMAI), Education Office**

| C3 Disciplinary Focus | C3 Inquiry Focus | Content Topic |
| --- | --- | --- |
| Geography | Evaluating sources and using evidence | Environment |

**C3 Focus Indicators**

**D1:** Explain how a question represents key ideas in the field. (D1.1.6-8)

**D2:** Explain how the physical and human characteristics of places and regions are connected to human identities and cultures. (D2.Geo.6.6-8)

**D2:** Evaluate the influences of long-term human-induced environmental change on spatial patterns of conflict and cooperation. (D2.Geo.9.6-8)

**D3:** Develop claims and counterclaims while pointing out the strengths and limitations of both. (D3.4.6-8)

**D4:** Critique arguments for credibility. (D4.4.6-8)

**D4:** Assess their individual and collective capacities to take action to address local, regional, and global problems, taking into account a range of possible levers of power, strategies, and potential outcomes. (D4.7.6-8)

| Grade Level | Resources | Time Required |
| --- | --- | --- |
| 6–8 | Resources cited in chapter; NMAI website. | 2–3 days |

# Introduction and Connections to the C3 Framework

Many people think of American Indians only as historical figures, but we are still here, vital communities dealing with important contemporary issues of cultural, economic, and environmental sustainability.

—Kevin Gover (Pawnee), director, National Museum of the American Indian

Native peoples and cultures of the Western Hemisphere are intricately and deeply intertwined with the places and environments they have occupied for thousands of years. American Indians have a rich history of studying, managing, honoring, and thriving in their homelands—in environments from arctic tundra to deserts, and everything between. Complex knowledge systems resulted from long-term occupation of tribal homelands and observation and interaction with places. These foundations continue to influence

American Indian relationships and interactions with the land today. As modern people dealing with issues of environmental degradation, American Indians continue their stewardship of the environment.

In this geography lesson focused on the C3 Framework, students will conduct an inquiry into four diverse American Indian communities that are addressing serious environmental issues in their homelands today. Ultimately, this inquiry prepares students to take informed action with regard to their own environment. The primary study resource for these activities is an educational website created by the National Museum of the American Indian, titled "American Indian Responses to Environmental Challenges." (http://www. AmericanIndian.si.edu/environment) The website was developed by the NMAI in collaboration with the Akwesasne Mohawk of northern New York, the Campo Kumeyaay Nation of southern California, the Leech Lake Band of Ojibwe of northern Minnesota, and the Lummi Nation of Washington State. These communities represent four diverse histories, cultures, geographic locations and environments, and types of environmental issues. The website documents how the communities have responded to environmental challenges, using their traditional cultures, values, and knowledge in combination with contemporary science and technologies to inform and conduct their environmental work.

The annual First Salmon Ceremony affirms and perpetuates the Lummi Nation's time-honored connection to and respect for salmon. The ceremony is held at the Lummi Nation School, thus helping to educate the next generation of Lummi citizens to care for salmon. This is only one component of a comprehensive community strategy to address a serious environmental issue.

PHOTO BY KAT COMMUNICATIONS, NMAI, 2010

# Inquiry Arc

This C3 Inquiry lesson provides opportunities to understand environmental issues in the context of people's cultural, historical, and contemporary relationships to place, with the National Museum of the American Indian's special resources providing learning examples from Indian Country. In Dimension 1, students and teachers explore the compelling question for this inquiry—"Whose job is it to fix environmental problems?" In class discussions facilitated by the teacher, they dissect the question and begin to understand the complexity of issues involved. In Dimension 2, students delve deep into the inquiry by using rich media and interactive resources provided by the National Museum of the American Indian to analyze the long-standing relationship between four American Indian communities and their environments, the environmental problems they are facing today, the impact of those problems, and how, as communities, they are responding. In Dimension 3, students use the information they have garnered from their exploration of the American Indian case studies to build arguments with supportive evidence to answer the question. Students conclude their inquiry within Dimension 4 by answering the question: *Whose job is it to fix environmental problems?* Finally, students research and take some form of action on a specific environmental issue of their own community.

At first consideration, the question "Whose job is it to fix environmental problems?" may seem somewhat obvious or rhetorical. A teacher may want to focus students on an environmental issue that students face close to home. For example, in Washington, D. C., where there is a metropolitan population of over 5 million people, we encounter issues of protecting the important ecosystem of the Chesapeake Bay, located about 90 miles down the Potomac River. The bay is home to many species of birds, mammals, insects, reptiles, shellfish, and fish and produces about 500 million pounds of seafood per year. Its fragile ecosystem is challenged by numerous factors, including storm water runoff from the many cities and farms that comprise its watershed of 64,000 square miles.

Each of the four American Indian communities featured in this inquiry faces a unique environmental problem. Let's consider one of the four case studies to provide insight into the lesson's compelling question:

Members of the Lummi Nation of coastal Washington refer to themselves as "salmon people." Pacific salmon migrate thousands of miles up and down the northwest coast from California to Alaska. For millennia, the Lummi survived on various species of Pacific salmon as the fish migrated through Lummi waters. Not only did they survive on salmon as food, but Lummi culture is deeply tied to salmon through language, stories, arts, values, and ceremonies. The Lummi know and respect the lives and ways of salmon. With the arrival of Europeans and Americans, the advent of commercial fishing, and the growth of population and industrialization, the pressure on salmon steadily increased. A few decades ago, the Lummi noticed some big changes happening. Fewer and fewer salmon returned each year and the Lummi couldn't catch them as readily as they always had. Fewer fish were spawning in the rivers, meaning that fewer eggs hatched and turned into the salmon fry that migrate into the ocean. They also observed that the water temperature was increasing. They saw that salmon migration patterns changed as the fish sought cooler waters. The Lummi knew that salmon were in trouble. Salmon fishing is a huge international industry affecting millions of people. Scientists, commercial fishermen, and everyone somehow connected to salmon recognized the problem.

After a brief introduction to the salmon problem, teachers will want to facilitate a discussion among the students asking probing introductory questions to the larger inquiry: Whose job is it to try and fix the salmon problem? We recommend focusing on "responsibility" by asking students about individual roles in fixing the salmon problem. The following questions could help prompt the students to think more deeply about roles and responsibilities when dealing with environmental problems:

- Is it the job of people who created the problem?
- Is it the fishermen?
- Environmental polluters?
- People who eat salmon?
- People who live in areas that were once salmon habitat?
- The federal, state, or municipal governments?
- Is it Canada or the United States?
- Environmental organizations?

- Is it the Lummi and other Indian Nations of that region?
- Is it only adults, or is there a role for young people?
- What roles do educators, media personnel, or just average citizens play?

As students start to build out a responsibility matrix, the teacher should prompt them to think about how individuals and organizations might contribute to a solution but may be limited because of capacity or expertise. In doing so, students may also consider the following questions: Can large environmental problems be fixed by any one person or organization? Or, what is the broad spectrum of tasks and people needed to address an environmental problem?

Dimension 1 asks that students "explain how a question represents key ideas in the field." (D1.1.6-8) By allowing students some time at the beginning of the inquiry to deal with the thorny nature of environmental issues and fixing them, they begin their investigation with a curiosity about the ways in which others have dealt with this question.

| Who is responsible? | If so, how? |
| --- | --- |
|  |  |

## Dimension 2: Connections to Disciplinary Tools and Concepts

In Dimension 2, students will investigate four diverse American Indian communities that are addressing serious environmental issues in their homelands today. For this investigation, students begin with the question of "how." How do communities address environmental issues?

NMAI's educational website, "American Indian Responses to Environmental Challenges," serves as the primary resource for the Dimension 2 research. Four community stories are told through videos that were shot on location. For each of the four communities, there are five video segments:

- Meet the People
- About Our Homeland
- Our Environmental Challenge
- Our Strategies
- Our Future

A gallery of images and objects from the museum's collection provides additional visual support to the video stories. The site includes interactive features, numerous maps and other spatial representations, and discussion questions that help guide students through the exploration of the case studies.

In order to conserve time, teachers may wish to divide the class into groups, each group taking responsibility for a different case study. Remind students that they are analyzing these case studies in order to build a deeper understanding of the compelling question: Whose job is it to fix environmental problems? To take full advantage of the website resources, students should view the website's videos, use the interactive features, have group discussions, and take notes on their findings.

The following questions will help guide the case study explorations:

- What environmental issue is the American Indian community dealing with?
- What are some ways in which the environment is connected to this community's cultural traditions and people's identity? *For example, in the website videos, various Lummi people refer to themselves as "salmon people." What does that mean?*
- What is the environment like? *(land, water, climate, plants, animals)*
- What caused the damage to the environment? *Look at specific factors, historical to the present day.*
- What effects does the environmental damage have on the community's culture? Its economy? Other factors?
- What actions are being taken by the American Indian community to repair the damage to their environment? Who is involved, both inside and outside of the community *(i.e., partnerships)*? What kinds of things are they doing?
- What are this community's hopes for the future of its culture and environment? *Remember, hope is a good motivation for action.*

In answering these questions, students are practicing the C3 disciplinary skills outlined in the geography section of Dimension 2. Students will work to "explain how the physical and human characteristics of places and regions are connected to human identities and cultures" (D2.Geo.6.6-8) and to "evaluate the influences of long-term human-induced environmental change on spatial patterns of conflict and cooperation." (D2.Geo.9.6-8)

## Dimension 3: Evaluating Sources and Using Evidence

Students can now begin organizing their findings and working with additional sources to construct arguments to answer the question, "Whose job is it to fix environmental problems?"

An effective argument is backed by evidence, and students should be prepared to support their conclusions and claims with data from the case studies. For example, students might wish to make a statement such as "The people of the Lummi Nation have a strong cultural connection to the salmon and, therefore, believe they must assist in fixing the salmon problem." What is the evidence that supports this conclusion? Students should cite specific references to the resource materials. For example:

- Felix Solomon, Lummi artist and former commercial fisherman:  "Well, we fished for thousands and thousands of years, you know, so salmon is a main staple of our diet, and always has been and still is very important. It's a food that satisfies your spirit inside. It's our identity here in Lummi—we're salmon people." [**Lummi Nation, Meet the People, video, 1:23.**]

- The traditional story, "The Bear and the Steelhead," teaches the Lummi people to be respectful of earth's gifts, such as the salmon. [**Lummi Nation, About Our Homeland, Try These Questions**]

Additionally, the students' investigation might lead them to make claims, such as "American Indians are solving big environmental issues that require many people working on many different kinds of jobs." They should be able to cite evidence from their inquiry that leads to this claim. For example, here are some of the many activities cited on the website that the Lummi Nation and their partners are taking to support salmon restoration:

- Repairing water habitat by creating engineered logjams
- Growing and replanting trees in the river watersheds
- Decreasing erosion and deforestation by installing road culverts and managing logging
- Decreasing ground and water pollution from farms and urban development
- Operating fish hatcheries to supplement the wild fish population
- Managing and enforcing commercial fishing rules and regulations
- Creating and enforcing laws that support the salmon recovery effort
- Managing data and records
- Educating the public about the need for salmon recovery efforts
- Educating youth and getting them involved

Dimension 3 is a critical organizational step in the inquiry. By working with claims and evidence to support those claims, students are practicing the C3 inquiry skills, "Develop claims and counterclaims while pointing out the strengths and limitations of both." (D3.4.6-8) Ultimately, students should emerge from these exercises feeling confident that they have all the information and documentation they need to answer the question, "Whose job is it to fix the environment?"

## Dimension 4: Communicating Conclusions and Taking Informed Action

Dimension 4 of the Inquiry Arc encourages students to communicate their conclusions (synthesize) and to take informed action (apply) to address a local environmental problem. More specifically to this lesson, they begin to demonstrate a more respectful way of living in relationship with an environment.

### COMMUNICATING CONCLUSIONS

The first task is for students to communicate what they have learned from the American Indian case studies. How did the American Indian communities themselves answer the compelling question of "Whose job is it to fix environmental problems?" Each student group should prepare and provide an oral or multimedia report for the rest of the class on the American Indian community they chose to study. This will ensure that all students have the opportunity to learn about all four communities. Their reports should cite the evidence for their conclusions.

Subsequently, the class could engage in a discussion or a debate on their findings using critical lenses to assess the various ways in which communities might best approach an environmental problem. Teacher-facilitated discussion will help draw out the most salient issues and help students make comparisons and contrasts among the community stories. In doing so, teachers should encourage students to "critique arguments for credibility." (D4.4.6-8)

In the final step of this inquiry students launch a community project of their choice to help improve environmental conditions in their area. Teachers can anchor this experience with the following call for individual action:

> You have got to take responsibility. It doesn't matter what the next person does or doesn't do. It's about what you do. And that's really important.
>
> —Maxine Cole (Mohawk), Teacher, Akwesasne Freedom School

With the help of teachers, students will research and assemble resources that allow them to construct a picture of their own community's environment and its well-being, develop a plan, and take civic action. Just as they did in the inquiry above, students will need to "assess their individual and collective capacities to take action to address local, regional, and global problems, taking into account a range of possible levers of power, strategies, and potential outcomes." (D4.7.6-8)

To that end, students should locate maps, photos, newspaper articles, videos, and other resources. They could interview community members, conduct public opinion surveys, or attend public meetings where environmental issues are being discussed. The following questions build on those discussed in Dimension 2 to focus students on their own community:

- What environmental issues are we dealing with in our community?
- What is the environment like where we live?
- How are our cultures, identities, and economies formed by our environment?
- What factors have contributed to any environmental damage where we live?
- How are people working to repair the damage to our local environment? Who is involved, and what are they doing?
- What are our hopes for the future of our environment?

Educating others and raising awareness of important issues is a form of civic action. Encourage students to share what they have learned. They'll be making an important contribution to the community's effort, and by now, they will understand how big jobs like fixing the environment get done. Encourage them to share with other students, community organizations or leaders, the local newspaper or other media, and others.

A poster-making tool is provided on the website "American Indian Responses to Environmental Challenges." Students can use it to create a poster online and download it to a classroom computer. It can also be posted on the website (http://www.AmericanIndian.si.edu/environment)!

# About the National Museum of the American Indian

The National Museum of the American Indian (NMAI) is one of 19 Smithsonian Institution museums and galleries. The NMAI mission is to advance knowledge and understanding of the Native cultures of the Western Hemisphere—past, present, and future—through partnership with Native people and others. The museum works to support the continuance of culture, traditional values, and transitions in contemporary Native life. Through its national education work NMAI is striving to improve the depth and quality of instruction about Native peoples in K-12 schools throughout the United States.

For essential resources to support this lesson, please visit:
http://www.AmericanIndian.si.edu/environment

For additional information and educational materials in the social studies and other disciplines, please visit: http://AmericanIndian.si.edu/education

*The author of this chapter is Edwin Schupman, Education Product Developer at the National Museum of the American Indian. The copyright of this chapter is owned by Smithsonian/National Museum of the American Indian. ©2014 Smithsonian/National Museum of the American Indian.*

# Are The **Principles** of The U.S. Constitution Reflected in Your School?

**National Constitution Center**

Constitution Day 2014 at the National Constitution Center, Philadelphia, Pennsylvania.

NATIONAL CONSTITUTION CENTER

### National Constitution Center Education Department

| **C3 Disciplinary Focus** | **C3 Inquiry Focus** | **Content Topic** |
|---|---|---|
| Civics | Applying disciplinary tools and taking informed action | U.S. Constitution and school government |

**C3 Focus Indicators**

**D1:** Explain how the relationship between supporting questions and compelling questions is mutually reinforcing. (D1.4.6-8)

**D1:** Explain how supporting questions contribute to an inquiry and how, through engaging source work, new compelling and supporting questions emerge. (D1.4.9-12)

**D2**: Analyze ideas and principles contained in the founding documents of the United States, and explain how they influence the social and political system. (D2.Civ.8.6-8)

**D2**: Apply civic virtues and democratic principles when working with others. (D2.Civ.7.9-12)

**D3:** Identify evidence that draws information from multiple sources to support claims, noting evidentiary limitations. (D3.3.6-8)

**D3:** Identify evidence that draws information directly and substantively from multiple sources to detect inconsistencies in evidence in order to revise or strengthen claims. (D3.3.9-12)

**D4:** Apply a range of deliberative and democratic procedures to make decisions and take action in their classrooms and schools, and in out-of-school civic contexts. (D4.8.6-8)

**D4:** Apply a range of deliberative and democratic strategies and procedures to make decisions and take action in their classrooms, schools, and out-of-school civic contexts. (D4.8.9-12)

| **Grade Level** | **Resources** | **Time Required** |
|---|---|---|
| 6–12 | Resources cited in the chapter; National Constitution Center website | 2–3 days |

# Introduction and Connections to the C3 Framework

Having students use constitutional concepts to analyze school policies and practices is a promising approach that can promote school improvement and cultivate the next generation of active citizens. Students can gain a greater sense of agency and belonging, and support a wide range of academic and social competencies, through involvement in the creation, implementation and review of school policies and practices, including discipline codes, curriculum, instruction and assessment. The involvement of students in school leadership also helps to cultivate more democratic, socially just institutions.

The National Constitution Center has developed a series of lessons and an innovative, research-based, youth-adult school governance model called *We the School,* to help cultivate democratic leadership and civic instruction in schools. This chapter expands one of these lessons: *Are the principles of the U.S. Constitution reflected in your school?* The lesson is designed to enrich students' basic understanding of core constitutional concepts in order to examine the democratic nature of their school. The lesson encourages students to examine constitutional concepts as they evaluate school policies and practices. Through the careful consideration of specific constitutional concepts, students will come to better understand why certain concepts are enacted in their school and why others are not. Students will examine the following constitutional concepts in their research and analysis.

- Checks and balances
- Separation of powers
- Independent judiciary
- Rule of law
- Amendment process
- First, Fourth, and Fifth Amendment rights

After inquiring about how the Constitution is applied in their school, students will communicate their findings and produce an action plan that will address ways in which they can affect school policy.

# Inquiry Arc

## Dimension 1: Developing Questions and Planning Inquiries



The lesson presented in this chapter provides students an opportunity to inquire about how we can create a safe and successful educational environment that follows on Justice Brennan's notion of school as a civic space without trampling students' rights. Specifically, this lesson provides students an opportunity to examine constitutional concepts, as applied in a school setting, to provide students with more voice in school policy and practices.

**EXAMPLES of** how we see the principles of the U.S. Constitution reflected in our school.

**WAYS** our school can incorporate some of the principles of the U.S. Constitution.

The compelling question informing this lesson is taken from the title of our *We the School* publication, "Are the principles of the U.S. Constitution reflected in your school?" Students should assess a dilemma many schools struggle to address, namely how can schools find an appropriate balance between order and liberty? Ask for one or two examples of constitutional principles reflected in their school and one or two examples of principles students would like their school to incorporate. At this point, you might even have students propose a preliminary answer to the question, "Are the principles of the U.S. Constitution reflected in your school?" (A model format for addressing such issues is the National Constitution Center's Town Hall Wall Poster, which summarizes an issue and presents arguments for each side. See http://constitutioncenter.org/the-exchange/exchange-educational-resources/classroom-resources.)

Extend the discussion by asking students to also consider if their school has been able to create a safe and successful learning environment with fair rules and regulations to guide administrators, teachers and students. Students should consider the entire school population when responding to this question rather than just their own experiences. Students might also discuss a specific policy or experience to illustrate their ideas.

After this initial work to establish the compelling question, facilitate students as they pose related supporting questions. The C3 Framework suggests that students should be able to "explain how the relationship between supporting questions and compelling questions is mutually reinforcing" (D1.4.6-8) and to "explain how supporting questions contribute to an inquiry." (D.1.4.9-12) Supporting questions might emerge from students considering the ways in which their school's rules sometimes protect the learning environment, but at other times might overstep constitutional boundaries. Some of these questions might include the following.

- What is due process and how does it apply to classroom and school management policies?

- How did the Supreme Court rule in *Tinker vs. Des Moines* on students' first amendment rights?
- What protections do citizens have under the 5th Amendment, and to what extent do those rights apply in schools?

## Dimension 2: Connections to Disciplinary Tools and Concepts

James Madison argued in Federalist No. 51 that "ambition must be made to counteract ambition." Borrowing the ideas of Montesquieu and other Enlightenment scholars, who believed that liberty rests upon the separation of different powers of government, Madison and the framers of the U.S. Constitution designed a three-branch system in which each entity would have its own powers, yet each would also have the ability to regulate the others. Checks and balances and separation of powers are concepts that undergird the design of the U.S. representative democracy that divides responsibilities across structures and roles, yet also facilitates intra-governmental cooperation. These concepts should frame students' analysis and evaluation of school policy and practices, and can be explored using a student worksheet. Indicator D2.Civ.8.6-8 in the C3 Framework reinforces these concepts in that students are expected to be able to "analyze ideas and principles contained in the founding documents of the United States, and explain how they influence the social and political system." Indicator D2.Civ.7.9-12 requires them to "apply civic virtues and democratic principles when working with others."

After distributing the worksheet, have students list examples of constitutional concepts they find in their school. Students should evaluate the appropriateness and presence of constitutional concepts in their school in order to deepen their understanding of these concepts. For example, on the worksheet students are provided an excerpt of Article I, Section 7 describing the concepts of checks and balances and separation of powers. Ask students: how are the policies of your school decided? Who is involved in the process? Students should identify examples to support their answers and then rank their school on a scale from 1-5 in terms of how well these concepts are reflected in the school's structure, policies, and practices. In other words, students should determine how school policies are decided, how inclusive that process is, and to what extent that process is monitored by others. Additional questions and related constitutional concepts for students to examine include the following.

- How does your school determine when rules are broken? Does the same person who makes the rules act as judge and juror? (Independent Judiciary and Rule of Law) Students might be able to find this information in school discipline and school board policy documents.

- Who has a say in changing the policies of your school? And how is that achieved? (Amendment Process)
- Do school policies violate a student's right of expression? (Individual Rights: Speech, Religion, Assembly, Free Press, and Petition)
- What provides just cause for an administrator to search and seize a student's property? (Searches and Seizures)
- Is there a fair process for challenging a rule or consequence for a student's behavior? (Due Process) If interested, students can discuss their due process rights by examining *Goss v. Lopez* (1974) and *Wood v. Strickland* (1975).

**LAW AND THE STUDENTS' POSITION IN SCHOOL**

The way schools operate today illustrates that we have a long way to go. Take for instance the infamous *Morse v. Frederick* (2007) case, where the Supreme Court upheld a school suspension of a student that held up a "BONG HiTS 4 JESUS" banner during an off-campus activity during school hours.

Dissenting, Justice Stevens wrote, (the majority opinion) **invites stark viewpoint discrimination….it upholds a punishment meted out on the basis of a listener's disagreement with her (principal) of the speaker's viewpoint… the Court's ham-handed, categorical approach is deaf to the constitutional imperative to permit unfettered debate, even among high-school students, about the wisdom of the war on drugs or of legalizing marijuana for medicinal use.**

Stevens continued, **"If Frederick's stupid reference to marijuana can in the Court's view justify censorship, then high school students everywhere could be forgiven for zipping their mouths about drugs at school lest some 'reasonable' observer censor and then punish them for promoting drugs."**

Justice Stevens' criticism does get to the heart of the matter. Does the censorship of such conversations unfairly privilege one set of views over another and create an atmosphere of distrust between students and administrators? Frederick was not even using drugs. Yet, court decisions encourage administrators and teachers to bypass conversations about students' social, cultural, and economic challenges and instead just punish students through the legal system.

## Dimension 3: Evaluating Sources and Using Evidence

Given their analysis of school policies, students should begin to make some inferences about the relevance of constitutional concepts to their school's policies and practices. This process requires that students "identify evidence that draws information from multiple sources to support claims, noting evidentiary limitations." (D3.3.6-8) There will be different interpretations of the evidence, so that students will need to "detect inconsistencies in evidence in order to revise or strengthen claims." (D3.3.9-12)

1. Use these questions to support students as they consider the constitutional nature of their school policies and procedures.
2. Why would you want constitutional concepts articulated in your school?

3. Consider positive outcomes the framers envisioned when drafting the U.S. Constitution, such as a system of checks and balances and individual rights.

4. In your opinion, what are some negative outcomes of having these concepts drive policies in your school?

5. Consider questions such as, "Can students be trusted to govern?" and "Should schools be more democratic?"

6. Do you feel, as a student, that your voice is heard and represented in your school system?

7. Use the Student Worksheet for reference.

8. Are there policies in your school that violate your right to due process? Searches and seizures? Freedom of expression?

9. Refer to the Student Handbook or equivalent book of school policies for reference. Consider examples such as a student dress code, right to assemble, and punishment for violating school policy.

10. Are there policies in your school that violate your right to due process? Searches and seizures? Freedom of expression?

11. Refer to the Student Handbook or equivalent book of school policies for reference. Consider examples such as a student judicial review system, the role of the student council, etc.

12. In your view, are the principles of the U.S. Constitution reflected in your school? Explain your answer.

13. Students should use evidence and examples that were previously listed to support their answers.

Students should be expected to take a position on the compelling question and to support their claims with evidence. For example, is it appropriate to create a system of checks and balances in the school's governance system when creating new policy? Should students have an ability to challenge a rule they view as unjust? Could such a process help or hinder the school environment? What would that look like? As such, this lesson can be a springboard for students' further investigation into the ways in which their school both espouses and practices the cultivation of democratically engaged communities, and the ways in which school policies and practices might be intentionally or unintentionally undermining or encouraging active citizenship.

## Dimension 4: Communicating Conclusions and Taking Informed Action

Dimension 4 asks students to "construct arguments using claims and evidence from multiple sources, while acknowledging the strengths and limitations of the arguments" when creating action plans. (D4.1.6-8) Are the principles of the Constitution reflected in our school? Should they be? If so, what might that look like? Is the current process in which school policy is made, implemented and reviewed effective? Could constitutional principles and processes strengthen policy and practice? After assessing the presence and appropriateness of constitutional concepts in their school, students should begin the process of establishing ways to communicate their findings and ideas to peers, faculty, staff, and administrators.

*We the School* provides an innovative youth-adult governance model that enables students to communicate their conclusions and take informed action. Such a process requires students to "apply a range of deliberative and democratic procedures to make decisions and take action in their classrooms and schools, and in out-of-school civic contexts." (D4.8.6-8; a similar objective is also outlined in D4.8.9-12.) Students can engage with this model by answering the above questions. There may be overlap for certain examples, such as a policy that reflects a constitutional concept but may also need revision in the student's opinion.

Students can also share the rankings they developed of their school's policies and come to a consensus for each finding as a group. They might even ask themselves the question: "Is change necessary?"

To take informed action, students can create a Plan of Action if they find their school is falling short in some aspect of policy. They might also form a committee to review the role of student government in the school, asking questions such as: Are the students' voices considered when drafting school policies and curricula? Is your student government only responsible for planning and organizing important student events and extra-curricular activities? Students might even draft a new school constitution.

Student government leaders—who often do not have a voice in school decisions—rarely serve as true partners in shaping how schools are governed. The *We the School* program is a model for youth-adult governance that helps address that gap. *We the School* serves as a how-to manual for schools that wish to make such a transformation a reality, and can be used by faculty, administrators and students to create an action plan that makes the most sense for their school and community. This lesson can be an avenue to begin such a process.

# About the National Constitution Center

The National Constitution Center in Philadelphia is the Museum of We the People, America's Town Hall, and a Headquarters for Civic Education. As the Museum of We the People, the National Constitution Center brings the United States Constitution to life for visitors of all ages and inspires active citizenship by celebrating the American constitutional tradition. The museum features interactive exhibits, engaging theatrical performances, and original documents of freedom. As the only institution established by Congress to "disseminate information about the United States Constitution on a non-partisan basis," the National Constitution Center serves as a Headquarters for Civic Education—offering cutting-edge learning resources, including the premier online Interactive Constitution. As America's Town Hall, the National Constitution Center hosts timely constitutional conversations uniting distinguished leaders, scholars, authors, and journalists from across the political spectrum. For more information, call 215-409-6700 or visit http://constitutioncenter.org.

*This lesson was created by the National Constitution Center Education Department and Marc Brasof.*

# CHAPTER 15

# Why **Vote?**

## Understanding Elections, The Candidates, and Why Any of This Matters

**Mikva Challenge**

Young men marching from Selma to Montgomery, Alabama in 1965 to demand voting rights.
PHOTO BY BRUCE DAVIDSON, ACCESSED AT HTTP://WWW.LOC.GOV/PICTURES/ITEM/2009631181

**Mikva Challenge Center for Action Civics**

| **C3 Disciplinary Focus** Civics | **C3 Inquiry Focus** Taking informed action | **Content Topic** Campaigns and elections |
| --- | --- | --- |

**C3 Focus Indicators**

**D1:** Explain how a question reflects an enduring issue in the field. (D1.1.9-12)

**D2:** Analyze historical, contemporary, and emerging means of changing societies, promoting the common good, and protecting rights. (D2.Civ.14.9-12)

**D3:** Gather relevant information from multiple sources representing a wide range of views while using the origin, authority, structure, context, and corroborative value of the sources to guide the selection. (D3.1.9-12)

**D4:** Construct arguments using precise and knowledgeable claims, with evidence from multiple sources, while acknowledging counterclaims and evidentiary weaknesses. (D4.1.9-12)

**D4:** Assess options for individual and collective action to address local, regional, and global problems by engaging in self-reflection, strategy identification, and complex causal reasoning. (D4.7.9-12)

| **Grade Level** 9–12 | **Resources** Resources cited in this chapter; Mikva Challenge website; chart paper, sticky notes, handouts, markers | **Time Required** 1 week |
| --- | --- | --- |

# Introduction and Connections to the C3 Framework

We've all seen the dire news stories about youth voting statistics and youth civic knowledge.

We know these statistics, but we also know that young people aren't apathetic. They care deeply about their communities, and—if we give them the opportunity—they want to have a voice in how their communities are run. As an organization, we see this first hand from our work with Chicago youth over the past 14 years. In 2008 and 2012, our city's youth provided a glimpse into their civic power through their efforts to increase voter turnout and the subsequent impact on the outcome of those elections. We know the civic power of youth. The question is: Do schools know this? Are they doing enough to prepare our youngest citizens for an active and engaged civic life?

Mikva Challenge believes that the best way for young people to learn how to participate in a democracy is to actually participate in our democracy. Our motto is "democracy is a verb!" Mikva Challenge's action civics curriculum builds the foundational beliefs that:

- Young people possess valuable expertise on issues that concern them.
- Young people deserve an opportunity to have their voices heard.
- Civic learning happens best through inquiry, action, and reflection.

The C3 Framework advances Mikva Challenge's foundational beliefs by engaging students in the questioning, investigating, communicating, and action required of citizens in a democracy. The lessons detailed in this chapter are drawn from our Elections in Action curriculum, which is available online free of charge at http://www.centerforactioncivics.org/elections-in-action-lessons/.

Young men marching from Selma to Montgomery, Alabama in 1965 to demand voting rights.
PHOTO BY BRUCE DAVIDSON, ACCESSED AT HTTP://WWW.LOC.GOV/PICTURES/ITEM/2009631181

# Inquiry Arc

This chapter shows how to guide students through a C3 Inquiry focused on the electoral process and the powers an individual and groups of individuals can have on the outcome. First, students engage with the compelling question of "Why vote?" by exploring an iconic image that chronicles the struggle for civil rights in the 1960's. Next, students explore elections through the lens of relevant issues students identify as most important to them as they work through a series of learning stations. Then, students engage in research by evaluating sources to find out more about the candidates running for office and uncover the reasons why people do and don't vote. Students conclude their study with an opportunity to take informed action, including registering voters, the creation and dissemination of a Voter Education Guide, and campaigning for candidates.

### Dimension 1: Developing Questions and Planning Inquiries

While experience has proven to us at Mikva Challenge that students care deeply about issues in their community, students do not automatically see the value in leveraging elected office in order to bring about change. In fact, voter apathy and disengagement is common across the U.S., not only with youth.

To jump start an investigation into why voting matters and how it can be a powerful force for social and political change, students need to see why any of this matters. Begin the class's exploration of "how a question reflects an enduring issue in the field" (D1.1.9-12) by

| What I see. | What it represents. |
| --- | --- |
|  |  |

sharing a compelling photo such as the one at the beginning of this chapter (http://www.loc.gov/pictures/item/2009631181), and having students complete a T-chart in which they describe what they see in as much detail as possible in one column and what they think it represents in the other column.

According to the image, people were clamoring for this right in the 1960s. Using the T-chart as a springboard, engage students in a discussion using prompts like:

- Was that the first time voting rights were a problem?
- Was that the last time?
- Why does this issue of voting rights persist (endure)?

Ultimately, move students toward the compelling question: Why vote? Prompt students to think about why it does/does not matter and keep track of student responses on a graphic organizer like the one below:

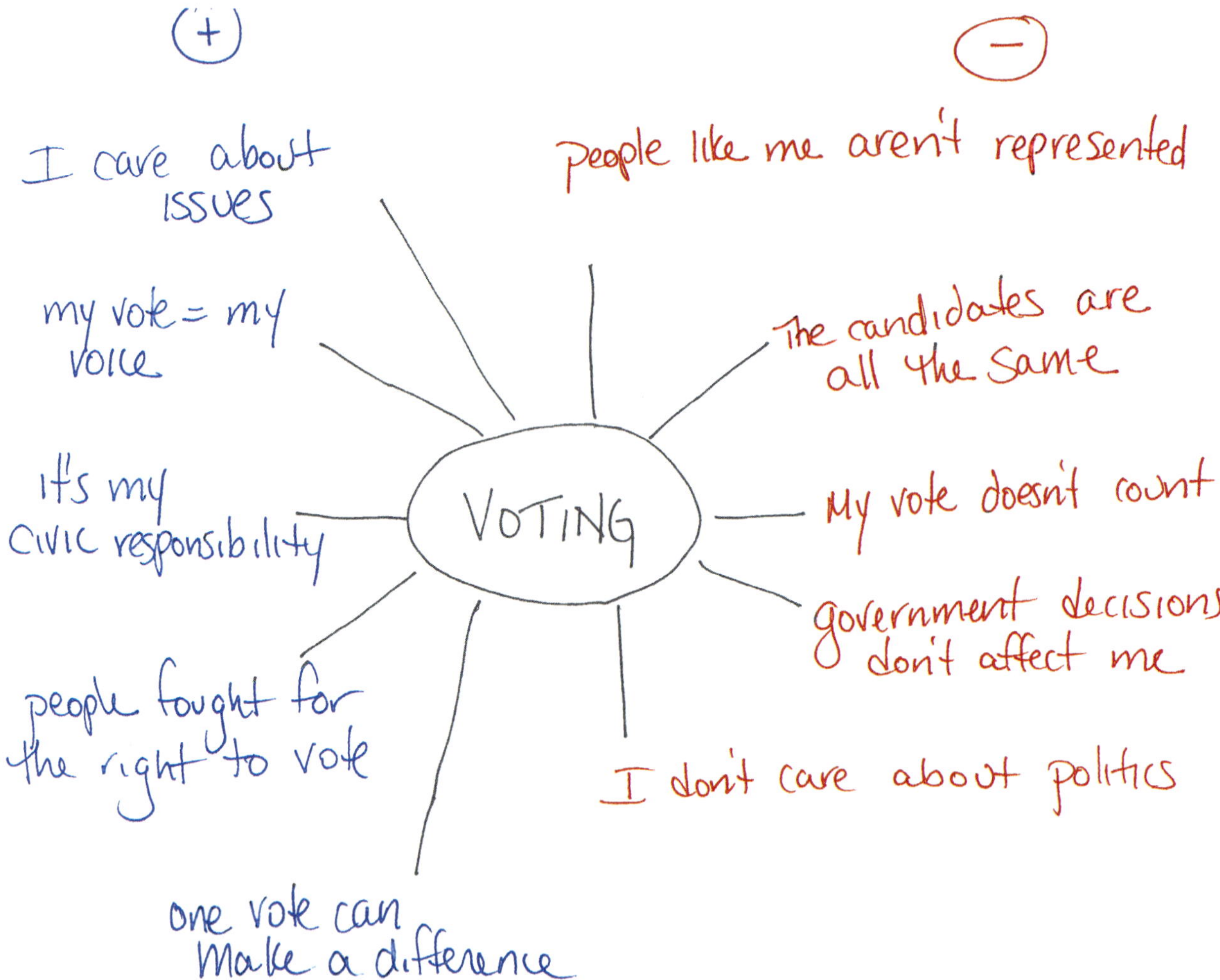

The following exercises help students dig deeper into the question framed in Dimension 1: Why vote? The classroom is set up in learning stations where, in small groups, students are given time to explore each response and then rotate through all the stations. Suggestions for learning stations should include, but are not limited to:

**LEARNING STATION 1: I vote… because I care about issues.**

To examine this statement, students read about a small town in Texas, as documented in "An Act of Faith in America" by Michael Seifert, where the Mexican American community that was previously ignored and neglected by their local government brought change to their community through a targeted increase in voting (See the This I Believe Essay online at http://thisibelieve.org/essay/989/). This narrative provides a tangible example of how a community used elections to induce change around specific issues. After discussing how the residents of the town brought about change through voting, students can choose an issue that they feel strongly about and brainstorm ways in which elected office could have an impact on that issue.

**LEARNING STATION 2: I vote… because the candidates running for office represent different points of view.**

To counter the belief that "it doesn't matter who gets elected; they're all the same," students compare two or more candidates' positions on issues. Depending on when in the year this lesson is taught and whether there is a competitive election taking place, students can either compare two or more candidates who ran against each other or are currently running against each other.

For example, Ralph Nader's 2000 run for president provides a good historical case study to examine. Many of his supporters claimed that there was little difference between the Democratic candidate, Al Gore, and the Republican candidate, George W. Bush, but if you examine Gore's and Bush's policies side by side, students can see that there was a great deal of difference (http://www.archive.ontheissues.org/Boston_debate.htm). Students should read the positions of the two candidates and complete a Venn Diagram that compares the two candidates. If the lesson is being taught during a competitive election, you can go to resources like www.projectvotesmart.org or www.ontheissues.org and print out current candidates' positions on the issues and have students complete a Venn Diagram.

**LEARNING STATION 3: I vote… voting is a right.**

At this learning station, students write individual reflections on Hosea Williams' (1965) quote "If you can't vote, then you're not free. And if you ain't free, children, then you're a slave" and discuss their thoughts with their group members. Students examine images of Black voters attempting to register to vote in the South under Jim Crow (http://tinyurl.com/895d8ca; http://tinyurl.com/ovj2wp7; http://tinyurl.com/q55uawx) as well as images of voters waiting in long lines in Ohio during the 2004 election (http://tinyurl.com/keceof9; http://tinyurl.com/oovlcry; http://tinyurl.com/n4ud6ez) and answer the question "If voting weren't powerful, why would people be denied that right throughout history?"

The learning station activities link the questions/issues that students raised in their discussion of why citizens vote in Dimension 1 to tangible civic content. Specifically, students practice "analyzing historical, contemporary, and emerging means of changing societies, promoting the common good, and protecting rights." (D2.Civ.14.9-12) A teacher may choose to add learning stations to specifically address questions/concerns students may have raised in Dimension 1 that are not represented here.

### Dimension 3: Evaluating Sources and Using Evidence

Deepening the discourse in response to the question "Why vote?" is the question, "Why don't people vote?" This question goes to the root of voter apathy and civic disengagement. First, students examine demographic data of who votes and who doesn't using census data of voter turnout for the last few elections (Access this census data online: http://www.mikvachallenge.org/wp-content/uploads/2014/09/C3_Elections_Lesson-3.pdf). Then students examine this foundational question by surveying voting aged members of their community to find out whether they voted in the last election and why (Access a sample survey tool online at: http://www.mikvachallenge.org/wp-content/uploads/2014/09/C3_Elections_Lesson-3.pdf). This form of primary action research illustrates the many ways students can gather data to build claims that answer a compelling question. In this way, students themselves can be social scientists. Assigning students to survey their own community not only builds their research skills (e.g., how to gather reliable data) and communication abilities, but engages students directly with their community.

Once students compile their data, they assess whether the prevailing cause of voter turnout is one of misinformation, apathy, disengagement, distrust, or some other reason. They begin to ask deeper probing "why" questions: Why don't people trust government? Why do people feel disengaged? Students then disaggregate their survey data by age, gender, and race and ask even more probing questions regarding who votes and who doesn't. How does their data compare with the census data? The survey enables students to "gather relevant information from multiple sources representing a wide range of views…." (D3.1.9-12) to inform their understanding of why people do/don't vote. They then begin to develop conclusions about the relationships between voter demographics, election results, and subsequent policy decisions—more evidence to develop a conclusion to the compelling question, "Why vote?"

### Dimension 4: Communicating Conclusions and Taking Informed Action

The sweet spot of action civics lies in Dimension 4—Communicating Conclusions and Taking Informed Action. Up to this point, the lessons detailed above exist as solid and thoughtful ways to teach about campaigns and elections. What they fail to do, without Dimension 4, is engage young people in the political process in the present tense. Mikva Challenge believes that classroom learning without authentic application is a missed opportunity.

First, students need the opportunity to synthesize their research by communicating their conclusions. We suggest that students engage in a structured deliberation, a debate, or a written exposition in response to the original question of "Why vote?" Providing students the opportunity to "construct arguments using precise and knowledgeable claims, with evidence from multiple sources, while acknowledging counterclaims and evidentiary weaknesses," (D4.2.9-12) allows them the opportunity to communicate their position on the topic. Because their responses will vary and represent a range of positions, the class can engage in true civic dialogue where opinions can respectfully differ.

In addition, the reasons why students should care will vary (and perhaps some students will still argue passionately against caring), leaving the "so what?" remaining. In other words, "Even if I do care, what can I do about it?" Because authentic action should respond directly to an identified need—and students will identify different needs—the types of actions will vary. For example, if students identify a lack of interest in voting in their community as an issue, they might stage a voter registration and/or get out the vote campaign. If they identify a lack of clear information about the candidates, they might publish and distribute a voter education guide. In other words, they are not taking action simply for the sake of taking action; they are taking action to bring about change.

In addition, a key element in taking action is the student-driven nature of the action. Students should be the ones leading the action; however, teacher guidance and support is important. For example, teachers can provide structures and choices for students to operate within. Having students identify the need to address is a good starting place for the action phase. From there, students set goals for what they would like to accomplish. Goal setting templates that help students think through the viability of their goals (e.g., Is it achievable? Is it timely?) provide a great structure for this brainstorming. Students then develop action plans (again, templates provide support and scaffolding) and assign roles. Teachers can also provide examples of relevant actions for students to choose from. Some examples include:

**CREATING A VOTER EDUCATION GUIDE** for the school community and their community at large that addresses election basics (e.g., how to register, deadlines for registration) and/or carefully sourced information about the candidates running for office. A sample voter guide can be found at http://www.mikvachallenge.org/wp-content/uploads/2014/07/EIA_VOTERGUIDE2011.pdf

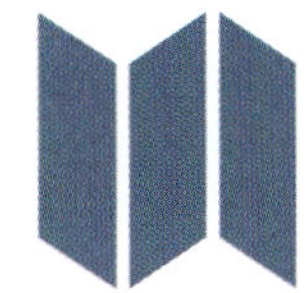

**CREATING A PUBLIC SERVICE ANNOUNCEMENT** (PSA) to raise awareness about the importance of voting or how to register to vote (sample PSAs are available at http://www.lwvil.org/voter-video-minutes.html).

**REGISTERING THEMSELVES AND OTHERS TO VOTE; ACTING AS AN ELECTION JUDGE.** While laws vary from state to state, there are usually ways for students to register themselves and others. In many states, students can also act as election judges. The League of Women Voters or your local Board of Elections can provide details. (See http://en.wikipedia.org/wiki/Student_Election_Judges).

**DIRECTLY CAMPAIGN FOR A CANDIDATE.** A key element of Dimension 4 comes by reaching beyond the classroom. Teachers and students collaboratively "assess options for individual and collective action to address local, regional, and global problems by engaging in self-reflection, strategy identification, and complex causal reasoning." (D4.7.9-12) Campaigning for a candidate can be a transformative experience for students. It is important for teachers to remain non-partisan and allow students to choose their candidates. Taking informed action should not be an activity that a teacher pre-arranged and simply has his/her students enact, as it is through the process of identifying needs, developing strategies, taking action, and reflecting on the action that students develop key problem solving, communication, and collaboration skills. It is this development of authentic leadership skills that makes Dimension 4 so powerful. For example, the creation of a Voter Education Guide or a PSA, without distribution in the community, is simply an academic exercise. The process of developing a plan for distribution (How will we get it printed? Where can we distribute it? Can we post it online? How can we drive traffic to our online posting?) offers great opportunities for students to problem solve, collaborate, and deliberate. These are the very same civic skills we are trying to build by teaching civics. By applying these skills directly, students have the opportunity to hone and develop them. Authentic informed action provides students the opportunity to see that what they are learning is relevant and powerful.

# About Mikva Challenge

Mikva Challenge is a nonpartisan organization founded in 1997 as a tribute to former White House Counsel, Judge, and U.S. Congressman, Abner Mikva, and his wife Zoe, a lifelong education activist. Mikva Challenge provides powerful learning opportunities for young people so that they can become informed, engaged citizens and community leaders. We accomplish this through our action civics programs that provide young people with authentic experiences in the democratic process. Working with teachers, we help students to reflect on their civic experiences; collaborate with other students to develop a "youth voice" on public issues; and grow into thoughtful, ethical, and inspired citizens.

Mikva Challenge's work has been showcased by scholars like Meira Levinson as the "gold standard" of action civics, a process in which youth voice is encouraged, valued and incorporated to the fullest extent possible; experiences, knowledge, perspectives, and concerns of youth are incorporated to the fullest extent possible; students learn by doing, with a focus on collective action; and student reflection and analysis is central to the process.

To receive a free copy of the full Elections in Action unit and learn more about our other action civics curricula, visit http://www.actioncivics.org or email cfac@mikvachallenge.org.

*The author of this chapter is Jill Bass, Director of Curriculum and Teacher Development at Mikva Challenge.*